Eventing Technique

Eventing Technique

Heinz von Opel

Translated by
Nicole Bartle

J. A. Allen
London

British Library Cataloguing in Publication Data
Opel, Heinz von
  Eventing technique.
  1. Eventing
  I. Title   II. [Military praxis]. *English*
  798.24

  ISBN 0–85131–533–X

First published in Germany in 1988 by Franckh'schen Verlagshandlung,
W. Keller & Co., Stuttgart

Published in Great Britain in 1991 by
J. A. Allen & Company Limited,
1 Lower Grosvenor Place, London SW1W 0EL.

© English translation, J. A. Allen & Company Limited 1991

Translator: Nicole Bartle
Additional editing: Jane Lake
Designer: Nancy Lawrence
Production: Bill Ireson
Typeset by Waveney Typesetters, Norwich
Printed in Great Britain by
St Edmundsbury Press Ltd, Bury St Edmunds, Suffolk

Contents

List of Illustrations

Line Illustrations

Foreword

The three-day event (or Military as it is called in Germany) has proved the versatility and endurance of the horse over the years it has evolved into an Olympic discipline. This has not detracted from its relevance; on the contrary, it is even more relevant to equestrianism now than it was in the past. With regard to the preservation of the horse, it has encouraged the selection of breeding stock that will pass on sturdy mental and physical health to its progeny. We must not allow the special natural qualities of horses: endurance, fighting spirit, courage and enjoyment of movement to deteriorate. The three-day event is a way of ensuring that those qualities are preserved.

Experienced riders have fostered the development of this special discipline. Their example determines the prevailing standard; it is they who, by trial and error, have learnt how to avoid hazards.

Not all successful riders in this discipline are able to pass on the secret of their success in a helpful manner to their followers. We should be all the more thankful to Heinz von Opel – who was a successful show-jumper before competing so successfully for ten years in the three-day event sport – for having recorded the result of his experience in this book.

Every counsel he gives reflects his expertise. In a systematic form, he explains to the reader how best to tackle every difficulty, from the walking of the course, through the dressage test, the important cross-country event and the final show-jumping test. Theoretical explanations are given only when they are absolutely relevant to the numerous practical tips. This is the strong point of this book.

Heinz von Opel knows what he is talking about. He is relating his own personal experiences during the course of his career as a three-day event rider. Training programmes complete this rich collection of personal experiences.

Every rider who wants to know how to get a horse fit for this event will find valuable advice in the following pages. Anybody who takes an interest in the sport will learn much by reading this book.

REINER KLIMKE

To my wife

Introduction

I was inspired to write this book when I realised how well my experience as a show-jumper had served me in coping with the difficulties that have to be surmounted during the cross-country phase of the three-day event. Twenty years experience of show-jumping since 1956 had obviously taught me some valuable lessons regarding the right approach to the uprights, spreads, and combinations, but also to water, walls and ditches like those included in the Hamburg-Derby showjumping course. I had learnt how to ride short and long distances between obstacles, to approach and to jump at an angle, to turn short and to ride on at speed.

Consequently the major part of this book consists of advice and tips regarding the approach to the various obstacles that have to be negotiated in the cross-country phase of the event. Of what use are a good dressage test and a clear round in the showjumping phase if the horse is likely to refuse at a jump into water or at a coffin? Only a small fraction of the obstacles on the cross-country course has been likely to pose problems for any of my horses. However this small fraction represents the challenge to me the rider: I am the one who must decide whether to check the speed or to drive on, who must decide on the rhythm, the angle of approach, the take-off point. Everything has to be right.

In the autumn of 1976 I finally decided to retire from show-jumping and to confine my sporting activity solely to eventing. I have trained approximately ten horses for this discipline and ridden them in many events, but the following lines and this book must be a memorial to one special partner.

At the Darmstadt-Kranichstein autumn sales in 1978 I was particularly interested in a four-year-old gelding that was the son of the thoroughbred Derby winner Alarich whom we had bred. The horse did not make a good impression in either the dressage test or the jumping test before the sale and consequently I was able to purchase him for very little money: his name was Akki

Bua. Akki Bua had to learn everything from scratch, but as a five-year-old, ridden by Willi Gayer, he performed with distinction in several competitions. One year later, I took him over myself. A win in a novice event was an encouraging beginning; what followed was an exemplary career. In nine years Akki Bua took part in 37 events, was placed 27 times and came first on 7 of those occasions. Together we must have negotiated around 500 cross-country obstacles, with only one fall and four refusals. However, only two of these refusals can really be counted as faults on the part of the horse, and they were committed when he was young and inexperienced.

We competed together for the last time at Achselschwang in 1987. At 13, Akki Bua is still perfectly sound. He may perhaps at some time in the future become a good schoolmaster over cross-country to my daughter Aline. I have gone into these details because my wonderful memories of partnering Akki Bua have given me two reasons for writing this book.

Firstly, I wish to encourage young riders of both sexes to take part in horse trials. At the beginning of his career, the horse need not cost a fortune. Nor is his training very time-consuming. My business commitments have never allowed me to devote more than an hour a day to the training of the horse. However he is allowed free exercise daily at pasture and, in addition, is hacked at a walk the day before an event. The important thing is to give the greatest attention to every detail, no matter how small, regarding every aspect of training for, and performance during, the competition. It is this attention to detail that has made three-day eventing the crowning achievement of equestrianism.

My other reason for writing this book is that there are in this discipline comparatively few competitive events in the course of a year. Horse and rider must therefore establish a very close relationship and a perfect accord during the period of training. In the case of a seven-year-old, I may sometimes wonder whether he was not at his best as a five-year-old. In the case of the 13-year-old Akki, I now know that it was at the age of 11, in 1985, that he had reached the highest point of his performing capacity.

What I also want to stress in this book, is that the beauty and the value of our sport reside not so much in the successes towards which we strive, but rather in the opportunity given to us during the training period to enjoy a special way of life, and of sharing this enjoyment in partnership with a horse.

In a totally different context, one of my tutors used to say: 'A path must always have an objective. But the most enjoyable part of reaching the objective is the path that leads to it.' I cannot think of a better motto for our beloved sport.

CHAPTER 1   The Training Programme

Success in all modern sports depends on methodical training. The necessity of meticulous preparation for competition is only slowly being recognised by participants in our particular sport, although it has been stressed for years in the writings of outstandingly successful competitors in Germany.

In the following chapters, I repeatedly emphasise the necessity of thorough planning and preparation of every phase of an event. The temperament and state of fitness of many event horses may need, for example, a slow, patient, well thought out period of preparation before the dressage test, of up to four to five hours sometimes, with frequent dismounting, mounting, riding, dismounting again. The cross-country course has to be inspected on foot several times; every obstacle, every variation of terrain, every curve of the course has to be studied, every moment planned so that you know within a few seconds where you will be at a certain time.

All this thinking and planning is not merely about getting the horse fit. The inexperienced horse must be methodically educated; a schedule of competitions must be set up for the whole year, and, finally, training for each particular competition must be planned in detail.

Schooling Plan

Training for eventing requires a lot of patience. Success depends essentially on the confidence and experience of both the rider and the horse. It is well known that a horse's fitness and jumping power play only a secondary role compared to experience and confidence when it comes to negotiating a relatively difficult coffin or jumping into water, cantering through water and jumping out again; or developing optimum speed, maintaining a regular cantering rhythm, and getting out of trouble in precarious situations.

Before going into the subject of schooling the young horse, I really must mention significant dates in Akki Bua's life, for his career appears to me to be a typical example of rational training.

He was born in 1974, and, as I have said, I bought him as a four-year-old in 1978, for the sole reason that my family had bred his sire, the thoroughbred Alarich.

As a five-year-old he took part in preliminary level dressage and novice showjumping competitions, and was twice successful in pre-novice horse trials. As a six-year-old he completed one long-distance ride, then two pre-novice horse trials and three novice ones. As a seven-year-old, he completed five novice events and was placed second in his first big competition at Wiesbaden-Kloppenheim. At eight he completed two short novice courses, two long ones (winning at Kloppenheim) and then took part for the first time in a short intermediate event.

As a nine-year-old he had four starts: a short novice, a more difficult novice (at Kloppenheim which he won), a short intermediate and his first international at Achselschwang where he was placed. As a ten-year-old he was entered in three events: a short intermediate, a tougher intermediate and an advanced. As an 11-year-old he completed four courses, coming third in an advanced event at Achselschwang. At 12, again he competed four times altogether and was seventh at Achselschwang. At 13 he started three times, twice in internationals (at La Valetta in Italy and at Achselschwang).

I recount all this only to show that a long, slow preparation and a progressive reduction in the number of competitions as the standard gets higher, get one further in the end than a policy of 'too quickly', 'too difficult' and 'too often'.

I will also repeat my advice that young horses should take part in novice and elementary dressage and showjumping competitions. Occasionally it can be beneficial for the older horse also.

Schooling Programme

The five-year-old
The horse can take part in novice dressage and newcomers' jumping competitions and the first novice horse trial can be contemplated and planned.

The six-year-old
If all has gone well up to now, you can plan the first three-day

event. You should not overlook the fact that the time allowed is about 15 per cent faster than in a one-day event (570 m per minute) and I would not, therefore, contemplate a long and difficult course. The inclusion of two roads and tracks and a steeplechase signify a considerable step up.

The seven-year-old

We can now contemplate our first big event but not yet one of the major championships. The physical and psychological strain would still be too great; you have to wait two or three years before venturing to take part in one of the really big events.

The eight-year-old

The eight-year-old horse is physically mature and can be faced with the difficulties of a major three-day event, but will still not have acquired a lot of experience. You must continue to have patience.

From nine to fourteen years old

This is probably the best time of life for the event horse. Lucinda Green says that the prime of life for the event horse is around 11 and 12 years, but it varies from horse to horse. Patience is still called for and a gradual building up of demands. As the demands become greater, the number of starts has to be reduced if the horse's soundness is to be preserved, and its competitive life lengthened.

| Tip 1 |

Patient and slow building up of demands is essential if one wants to prolong the horse's competitive life span.

The Yearly Plan of Events

The yearly programme of competitions has to be roughly drawn up in March at the latest, taking into account dressage tests, hunter trials, one-day events and showjumping competitions in which the horse can be entered between the eventing seasons.

You could reckon on two peak performances, one in June, the next in September. This gives six months in which to fit:

4–6 weeks fitness training;
the first trial;
a few days of relaxation;
1–2 weeks more intensive training;
the second trial;

a few days of relaxation;
2–3 weeks intensive training;
the first major event;
2–3 weeks holiday, i.e. very quiet work;
2–3 weeks normal training;
an intermediate trial;
some respite;
4–5 weeks fitness training before the major and hopefully decisive event of the year.

It is not always possible to stick strictly to this programme, but this is the general idea. Too long a rest period is as detrimental to the condition of horse and rider as an uninterrupted succession of taxing competitions.

The high points must depend on the state of education of the horse. With five- and six-year-old horses one could enter into two more or less easy two- or three-day trials in the course of the year. A seven-year-old or an older horse could possibly tackle two big events but I would never ride in more than six big events per year with the same horse. One-day events can be considered to be training trials. In his nine year career, Akki Bua took part in four major three-day events per year on average.

The Training Plan

A day by day training plan has to be established for each peak event. Preparatory training trials must of course be fitted into it. As an example I will now describe Akki Bua's programme from mid-April to the end of May 1987 in preparation for his first peak event, the medium three-day event at La Valetta.

The core of the plan is the interval training which I will explain in detail in the next chapter. This takes place every fourth day, but because of my professional commitments I would have to do it every third or fifth day. The intensiveness of demands in interval training is systematically increased. In the example cited above, we reached the maximum of three eight-minute sessions three weeks before the cross-country day at La Valetta; after this the intervals were reduced to three seven-minute sessions and then three six-minute sessions. After which, this fitness training would take place every other day.

The day after interval training I would do some dressage

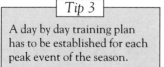

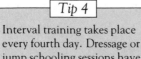

schooling, but I hardly ever go through the whole test prescribed; the horse learns only too quickly to anticipate the rider. I never allow an event horse to do a flying change in the course of this schooling. Flying changes are not required in dressage tests for eventers, but the counter canter is. I will, however, thoroughly work on halts, immobility, rein back, extensions, circles, voltes, half-pass, etc. I seldom do this dressage schooling in a marked-out dressage arena; an eventing horse is, and indeed must be, capable of doing all the movements in open country. Akki Bua has never liked hard grass, preferring mud, sand and most of all fetlock-high or even knee-high wet grass. In those conditions he wakes up, loosens up more quickly and goes with more impulsion. Young event horses particularly must be made to do dressage work frequently, perhaps every third day. I would submit Akki to strict dressage schooling only the day after interval training, thus twice in eight days.

The day after dressage, we do uphill work. Cantering uphill is wonderful gymnastic exercise for a horse. I attribute much of our success over the past years to our hilly home ground. There is no better way of developing the muscles of a horse's back and hindquarters than cantering uphill on the lightest possible contact. However, I vary this uphill work. On some days, after warming up at the foot of the hill for about 30 minutes, we do a number of short bouts of cantering up fairly stiff slopes for about five minutes, then walk downhill for ten minutes before repeating the exercise once more. On other days we will canter quietly up a more gentle slope for about eight minutes, with short interruptions, and then finish the exercise with a twenty minute walk home. There are many advantages to hill work: within the space of barely an hour the horse will have done a lot of walking up and downhill, which greatly develops his surefootedness. Besides this he will have developed his back and hindquarter muscles without straining the tendons. After a very few sessions, the horse will have become much calmer; his excessive energy will have been reduced. It is also good but not excessive work for heart and lungs. Finally it will have spared the horse's forelegs; there is no jumping, no speed, no risk of injury to tendons.

The day after the hill work we do some cross-country cantering at a much slower speed than in interval training (approximately 350 m per minute). I look for twisting courses, to teach the horse to canter in bends and turns at a regular speed. This is not fitness training as much as a lesson in staying on the bit at a prolonged canter; it teaches the horse surefootedness in varying ground conditions; it teaches him to accept changes of weight distribution in the turns and twists of the course. Although it is not interval training *per se*, I still work in intervals: 5–7 minutes canter, 3–4 minutes walk, two or three times depending on the stiffness of the course.

With Akki I do practically no showjumping practice at home; I occasionally make him jump a few isolated obstacles, especially combinations. Young horses on the other hand should frequently be faced with coloured obstacles and about every ten days be made to complete a whole course of obstacles. The obstacles need not be high; what matters is the regularity of the canter, a confident approach and calmness after the jump. I attach a lot of importance to gymnastic jumping: I do lots of bounce jumps, oblique approaches, jumping on a diagonal, often from the trot, and teach my horses to jump over water, into water, out of water, off and onto banks, for those small jumps which require considerable agility are usually more troublesome in competition than imposing ones which, in any case, can only be negotiated at speed.

Hacking is also part of the training; by hacking I mean active, long striding walking. All event horses have to be taken out of the stable twice a day. Because of my work, I have to ride very early in the morning, and devote an hour to an hour and a half to athletic training. In the evenings I go hacking at the walk. Even then I practise a form of interval training and especially before a major event I do some uphill work at the walk. An event horse can never be allowed a day of total inactivity, but once a week he can be given a respite from hard work. It may not be possible to exercise the horse regularly in the open air during the winter months, but from March to October there can be no Sabbath for horse and rider.

All my event horses, including Akki Bua, are turned out at grass every day for about four hours. There are many riders who hesitate to do this, for fear of 'grass injury'. The risk is small if the horse is always turned out with the same companions and is made to work every day under saddle. Leisurely movement in light and fresh air is good for the horse's nerves. Provided that they are fed

Tip 6
It is beneficial to his nervous system to turn the horse out to grass for at least one hour every day.

Day	Activity	Day	Activity
Mon.		Mon.	Interval training: 3×8 min canter
Tue.		Tue.	Dressage
Wed.		Wed.	Hill work
Thur.		Thur.	Hacking
Fri.	Cross-country canter work	Fri.	
Sat.	Interval training: 3×5 min canter	Sat.	Competition Birkenau
Sun.	Dressage	Sun.	
Mon.	Hill work	Mon.	Hacking
Tue.	Cross-country canter work	Tue.	Hill work
Wed.	Interval training: 3×5 min canter	Wed.	Interval training: 3×7 min canter
Thur.	Dressage	Thur.	Dressage
Fri.	Hill work	Fri.	Hill work
Sat.	Gymnastic jumping	Sat.	Cross-country canter work
Sun.	Interval training: 3×6 min canter	Sun.	Interval training: 3×6 min canter
Mon.	Dressage	Mon.	Hacking
Tue.	Hill work	Tue.	
Wed.	Cross-country canter work	Wed.	
Thur.	Interval training: 3×6 min canter	Thur.	Competition
Fri.	Dressage	Fri.	
Sat.	Hill work	Sat.	La Valetta
Sun.	Gymnastic jumping	Sun.	
Mon.	Interval training: 3×7 min canter		
Tue.	Dressage		
Wed.	Hill work		
Thur.	Interval training: 3×7 min canter		
Fri.	Dressage		
Sat.	Hill work		
Sun.	Cross-country canter work		

Akki Bua's Training Programme for the Three Day Event at La Valetta in 1987.

a sufficient diet of concentrates and are rationally trained, horses are less likely to gorge themselves on grass and develop a grass belly.

Feeding

A well-balanced diet has to be planned as well. It does not matter whether it is a diet of oats and hay or whether the concentrates are in the form of reliable commercially prepared cereal mixes. The important thing is to adjust progressively the nutritional value of the food to the physical demands made on the horse. It is equally important to cut down on the food after a competition. There are many excellent commercial brands of cubes on the market, specifically for race horses or competition horses, as well as vitamin and mineral supplements. The vet will advise you on the need to feed these supplements.

CHAPTER 2 Interval Training

All the members of my family took their sport seriously. It was for them a serious challenge rather than just a leisure activity. We constantly discussed ways of improving our performance. My father was a successful rowing athlete and would often discuss ways of improving the design of boats. It was he who first suggested that the coxswain be in a lying position. Thus, having showjumped for six years, I became interested in interval training, the method which had helped Scandinavian long-distance runners to the top of their sport. Briefly, the system consists of: stress – pause – stress. In the complete cycle, exertion is high at certain moments, without ever going beyond the bounds of safety.

My interest was spurred by reading Lucinda Prior-Palmer's book *Me and My Horse* in which she recounts how she had been told about interval training by the American eventing world champion Bruce Davidson; a system of fitness training applied to horses by the French trainer Jack Le Goff first in France and then introduced by him into the American eventing world. Lucinda has practised this system since 1974, since when she has become well known as a world champion. As I see it, interval training, is the superior method when compared with traditional methods, because the latter could induce me to continue galloping for an extra ten minutes even if my horse were not fit enough to sustain the strain on a particular day. The traditional fitness training method, involving long distances of relatively slow galloping, and some fast work, requires a lot of experience and a special feeling on the part of the rider. It does not provide a concrete appraisal of the condition of the horse at every step. It has another disadvantage in my eyes; even the keenest of horses can become bored during the long work-outs and start to trail its hindlegs. The load then falls entirely on the forelegs and their joints and tendons become severely stressed.

Interval training avoids those disadvantages. The short

| Tip 7 |
Interval training allows you to get a horse fit more accurately because the results can be constantly measured.

moments of stress make smaller demands on the horse's strength. During the intervals of respite, one can put the horse onto the aids again. In this respect I must quote the words of Dr. Bernd Springorum in his important book about the training of the eventing horse:

Middle distance running has been completely revolutionised by interval training. In this system the point where anaerobic work starts (the anaerobic threshold) is delayed, with the result that aerobic capacity is considerably augmented.

Stress within aerobic limits: the horse's capacity for intensive work increases without there being a build up of lactic acid.

Stress in anaerobic conditions: there is a quick build up of energy which is equally quickly dissipated. In those conditions lactic acid accumulates in the muscles and exhaustion sets in.

Interval training implies a systematic building up of aerobic capacity (elimination of lactic acid and renewal of energy by oxygenation of blood) to the extent that the body rarely if ever has to perform in anaerobic conditions.

At the beginning of interval training, I follow the programme described by Lucinda Prior-Palmer (now Lucinda Green).

1. There are always three intervals.
2. After every period of stress there must be a recovery pause of three minutes at the walk.
3. The speed of the canter during the periods of stress is 400 m per minute.
4. The length of the periods of stress is gradually increased, for example, at the beginning it can be three four-minute sessions; towards the end, approximately two weeks before the main event, it will be three eight-minute sessions. In the last two weeks the demands must be reduced to approximately three five-minute sessions.
5. Interval training should be carried out if possible every fourth day.

One can practise a milder form of interval training even with a five-year-old in preparation for a one-day event, for example, three three-minute sessions, then three four-minute sessions, and finally three three-minute sessions again.

For a short two-day event three five-minute sessions would be the top limit. For a long two-day event one could go up to three seven-minute sessions.

Three-day events obviously require harder training, but three ten-minute sessions should not be exceeded even in preparation for an international competition. One can, however, vary the length of the periods of walking and increase the speed of the canter.

My Personal Further Development of Interval Training

The particularly favourable training conditions which I enjoy at home, plus personal observation have led me to introduce a number of variations into the programme just described. They are:

- Flexible intervals of semi-rest.
- Varying the speed of the canter in the periods of stress.
- Keeping the horse constantly on the aids in the cantering intervals.
- Occasionally jumping some obstacles during the work-outs.
- Frequent monitoring of pulse and respiration.

Flexible periods of semi-rest

When I draw up the training plan, I decide from the beginning on which days interval training will take place and the length of the periods of stress. As shown in my 1987 programme in preparation of the three-day event at La Valetta, I started with three five-minute sessions to reach the peak of three eight-minute sessions after four weeks, and then cut down to three six-minute sessions in the last week. Akki was in top form in the event. He incurred no penalty points in the steeplechase, went round the cross-country course with ease in the fastest time and still had plenty of energy in reserve at the end. Since then I have never altered the programmed periods of effort but the periods of semi-rest have been kept flexible. Normally I accord the horse intervals at the walk of at least three minutes, but depending on pulse and respiration, they can be extended to four or five minutes. I consider this adjustment to be very important for one must take into account the daily form of the horse and other circumstances, such as a downpour of rain which suddenly makes the going heavy.

Changes of speed within the intervals of cantering
I always try to simulate to some extent the conditions normally prevailing in competition. For example I will use the same short stirrup length and the same bit. However, there is no cross-country course over which one can maintain the same uniform speed. Bends, narrow passages, up and down gradients constantly call for acceleration and deceleration and so I vary the speed during the work-outs. I will ride a number of tight S bends at a speed of approximately 300m per minute interspersing them with 20 to 30 cantering strides on the straight at 500–550m per minute. At the end of one interval or another Akki Bua knows the point at which he will be allowed to surge ahead at steeplechase speed. This always cheers him up enormously.

Keeping the horse firmly on the aids
Temperament or conformation makes some horses better at engaging their hindquarters than others, even over long periods of cantering; they are easy to keep on the aids. Not so Akki Bua, he prefers to go like a camel – better to devour the ground. To keep him rounded and on the aids is hard work. However the event horse must use its back for cantering and jumping, and it will only do so if it stays on the aids. It is extremely important therefore to develop its back muscles. Interval training allows me to keep Akki on the aids without getting exhausted myself; I consider it to be excellent for him and indeed essential gymnastic rather than just conditioning work.

Jumping obstacles in the course of the work-out
An important aspect of my interval training is the jumping of isolated obstacles in the course of the work-out. Of what use to the event rider is the supremely fit horse that charges at obstacles, will not slow down as it approaches a tricky combination (or only at the cost of a superhuman effort on the part of its rider) and that always jumps dangerously big into water? The aim in our sport is to complete the cross-country at optimum speed but as efficiently as possible, i.e. without waste of energy or effort. This can be the case only if rider and horse are always in perfect accord, so that every obstacle is approached at a controlled speed and jumped so nimbly that speed can be quickly restored as soon as the obstacle has been surmounted. The technique has to be

Tip 8

Interval training provides us
with the possibility of
simulating cross-country
jumping conditions.

acquired by constant practice which is ideally provided by interval training. The number of obstacles we jump in every work-out is very limited; the obstacles are neither high nor difficult and I always pay attention to the condition of the ground on both the approach and landing side. We may go over six obstacles per interval, which amounts to 18 obstacles in the day's work-out. However, I do very little of this jumping in the course of interval training if the horse is also undergoing a programme of gymnastic jumping.

The speed will vary considerably depending on the obstacle, from slow, to medium, to steeplechase speed. I avoid straightforward obstacles. Every obstacle must be of a particular type: in-and-out combinations of every variety, sunken ditches, walls, coffins, drop fences, etc. Akki has always had a strong aversion to white fences in open country. He may stop at them even on home ground. So I confront him with them from time to time, as well as with various jumps into water.

However once a particular obstacle has been negotiated, I will not ask the horse to jump it again. Repetition unnecessarily stresses a horse's forelegs. This means that I must change the obstacles in every work-out (which is the advantage of easily transportable cavalletti).

Is it too much to jump 18 obstacles every fourth day?
I consider that it is a proper compromise between consideration of the horse's soundness on the one hand and the need to give it useful experience on the other. The essence of the sport is the speediest possible coverage of a course of natural obstacles. Somehow we have to simulate the conditions we will meet in competition. I fully appreciate the practical difficulties of constructing suitable obstacles for interval training, especially since the obstacles must be varied, but where there is a will, there is a way, and I feel sure that the reader will be able to take the next step which is to plan and build obstacles that he can use in the course of interval training.

Monitoring of pulse and respiration
An essential part of interval training is monitoring the horse's pulse and respiration with the aid of stop watch and stethoscope. They give a more reliable indication of the state of fitness of my

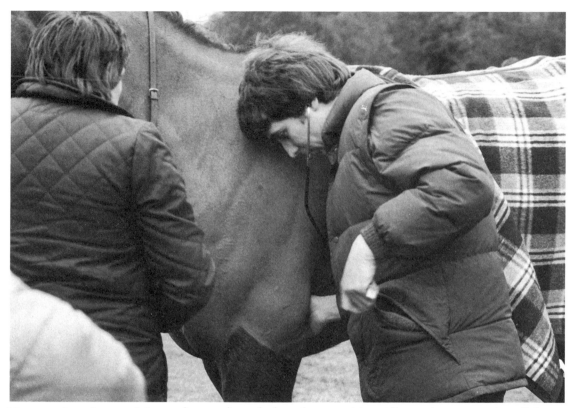

Measuring the pulse rate while counting the seconds on a stopwatch.

horse than feel and supposition. For quite some time I have attached great importance to the respiration rate. In Akki's case, at the end of the compulsory ten minute pause before the cross-country start in a medium event, his respiratory rate was 80 and his pulse rate well below 80. The vet had no hesitation in letting him carry on. In fact on this occasion Akki had not been able to give his best performance for he was suffering from catarrh, a problem, it was discovered later, caused by an allergy to hay.

It is of course necessary to know the normal pulse and respiratory rates of the horse at rest. The resting respiratory rate of horses is between 8 and 16 breaths per minute (10 in the case of Akki Bua) and the pulse rate between 30 and 50 beats per minute (36 with Akki). As a rule of thumb, it is considered that a horse has not been overstressed if pulse and respiration have returned to twice the resting rates within a period of ten minutes. As regards pulse rate, I agree; with Akki it would be down to 75 beats per minute after ten minutes, but I do not think that ten minutes is long enough for the respiration rate to come down to 20 after considerable exertion. My aim for Akki was a rate of less than 50 and this has always proved to be safe.

In any case the respiration rate should never exceed the pulse rate. If it does, one must stop work and the vet must be consulted.

Tip 10

Pulse and respiration have to be measured ten minutes after completion of the last interval. The figures allow you to find out how quickly the horse recovers from exertion and thus his state of fitness.

The pulse and respiration rates ten minutes after the last interval

These are the important rates. What distinguishes a fit person from an unfit one is not, for example, the rate of his breathing after running up a long flight of steps, but the shorter time in which his breathing returns to normal resting rate. A pulse rate of more than 80 or a respiration rate of more than 50 ten minutes after the last stress period are disturbing signs. The horse may be sickening. On the other hand it may just have been overstressed on the day, in which case the programme has to be adapted accordingly. Taking Akki Bua once more as an example, at the beginning of training for the 1986 three-day event at Achselschwang, ten minutes after a work-out his pulse rate was 75 or rather less, his respiration rate 50 or less. Both values became lower in the course of training. At the beginning of September, pulse rate was 75, respiration rate 40; by mid-September the respective figures were 60 and 30. So you know that your fitness training programme is sound if the figures ten minutes after the end of a work-out are within the right range or show a tendency to improve.

Respective rates at the end of the first interval

It is advisable at the beginning of training to measure the respective rates after the first period of stress. The rate of respiration can be measured by the rider himself. The pulse rate is better measured by an assistant with the aid of a stethoscope. The figures for individual horses vary. In the moment of maximum stress the pulse rate can be 240, the respiration rate around 150. With Akki, thirty seconds after the return to walk the pulse rate was never above 130, the respiration never above 100. In the ensuing weeks, there was no significant difference in the pulse rate after the first period. On the other hand the respiration rate steadily regressed to 90 at the end of three ten-minute intervals, and on the last day of training (three six-minute intervals) it was 80.

After two minutes

On the basis of the figures obtained immediately after the first period of stress, one can decide whether to proceed with the next interval of stress as planned after a pause of three minutes or, if the values are not completely reassuring, wait until the pulse rate has returned to 80 or less and the breathing to less than 70. With Akki Bua I have never had to wait more than four minutes. It would be a serious cause for concern if the respective rates were not much lower after two minutes than immediately after the end of the first period.

After the second interval

It is most significant that Akki Bua's respiration rate at the beginning of September and heart rate in mid-September were better at the end of the second period of stress than at the end of the first period. This is a clear sign of improving fitness as a result of training. However the greater 'motoring' capacity of heart and lungs requires a longer period of warming up. This is the point of the roads and tracks before and after the steeplechase in a three-day event. I had a bitter experience once with Akki. In the last third of his training period for a big three-day event (when we were doing three eight-minute sessions of interval training), I started him in a short two-day event, in which there was no endurance test (roads and tracks). This did not give the horse sufficient time to warm up. The beginning of the cross-country course was uphill and I took it at too fast a speed. Suddenly the horse started to tie-up; it had obviously started working anaerobically too soon and could not go much further. Just before what would normally have been for him a tiny hop out of water, Akki Bua came to an abrupt stop, paying me back for my foolishness by chucking me out of the saddle. However two weeks later he completed brilliantly an international three-day event which included a steeplechase phase.

After the third interval

The pulse rate immediately after the end of the third period of

Dates	Intervals 3×	Rates after 1st interval Immed. P/R	After 2 min P/R	Rates after 2nd interval Immed. P/R	After 2 min P/R	Rates after 3rd interval Immed. P/R	After 2 min P/R	Rates 10 minutes after 3rd interval Pulse	Resp.
27 Aug	6 min	115/75	100/75	120/80	90/50	120/90	100/80		
30 Aug	7 min	95/65	80/60	120/90	90/60	120/90	90/80		
3 Sept	8 min	90/85	80/75	100/80	90/75	100/90	90/80	75	40
6 Sept	9 min	95/70	90/65	110/65	85/55	120/75	90/60	75	50
9 Sept	10 min	100/90	90/55	100/60	85/60	100/80	85/60	70	40
13 Sept	9 min	110/85	90/70	105/65	90/55	120/80	90/75	75	30
17 Sept	8 min	100/85	90/65	95/80	85/55	100/65		60	30
23 Sept	6 min	90/80	90/65	90/72	85/55	100/60		55	30

Akki Bua's pulse (P) and respiration (R) rates; fitness training before Achselschwang August/September 1986.

stress is definitely weaker than after the first and second periods. The respiration rate however is lower. The motor has been properly warmed up. From the beginning of September onward, two minutes after the end of the third period the figures are no worse than after the first. Progress is satisfactory.

Conclusion

1. Careful monitoring of pulse and respiration is the most important aspect of interval training.
2. The total of pulse and respiration should drop by 50 per cent, ten minutes after a work-out.
3. Respiration rate should never be faster than pulse rate.
4. Do not start the next period of stress in a work-out before the pulse rate is 80 or less and the respiration rate well below this.
5. More satisfactory rates after the second and third interval are a good indication of enhanced condition. The motor has to be given more time to warm up.
6. The improvement must continue when the length of the periods of maximum stress is decreased in the two weeks preceding the main event.

CHAPTER 3 The Official Guided Tour of the Cross-country Course

Walking the cross-country course is one of the most enjoyable parts of the whole event. It is advisable, however, to stay at the head of the group of competitors; if you are caught in the middle you only get a vague impression of the obstacles and the line of approach.

William Steinkraus, the American showjumping champion of the Mexico Olympics in 1968, relates in his book *Riding and Jumping* how carefully he would pace a course; not only the distance between the elements of a combination, but also the distance between practically every single obstacle, be it ten or twelve canter strides, depending on the type of horse he was riding and the speed at which he planned to ride.

You have to familiarise yourself just as thoroughly with a cross-country course. Distances, changes of direction and ground conditions have to be carefully analysed and committed to memory like a piece of poetry: an uncommon feat of concentration of the mind when walking a course for the first time.

Instead of mingling with the happily chatting bunch of competitors with their accompanying dogs, I always try to walk as

much in front as possible so that I can see the ground and the obstacles coming towards me. I also try to stay close to the official who is guiding us. He often drops useful tips about the ground, about the peculiarities of certain obstacles and especially usefully may recount the experiences of previous competitors at those particular obstacles. When first walking a course, it is reassuring to hear that some rather formidable looking obstacle had to be jumped the previous year and that there were no casualties at that particular fence on that occasion. In addition I try to obtain advice from as many colleagues as possible who have already ridden over the course. The opinion of experienced riders as to whether a particular combination should be ridden in two or three canter strides is invaluable. One word from the mouth of an experienced competitor is often more helpful than long hours of cogitation.

Tip 11
Consult experts about the way to ride over a particular stretch of ground or to tackle individual obstacles; however, the final decision must remain entirely your own.

Driving Over the Roads and Tracks

As a rule it suffices to use a vehicle to inspect the roads and tracks, though some of the tracks are closed to motor vehicles and have to be covered on foot. Still it is important to examine carefully, and to remember, every square metre of the route. You cannot leave anything to chance and to casual observation; as in all the other phases of the event, the more thorough the preparation, the greater the chances of success.

Depending on the terrain, I decide in advance where to cover the ground at the walk, the trot or the canter. I plan the time of arrival at the end of phase A, allowing for a pause before the steeplechase. I may decide to ride some stretches at a rather greater speed than normal (for example 240 m per minute instead of 220) in order to be able to allow the horse a longer pause at the end. It is especially important to note every one of the compulsory check points along the roads and tracks. I have missed one out once at a major event; it is not an error that I am ever likely to repeat.

Inspecting the Steeplechase Course

You must walk the steeplechase from beginning to end at least once in order to become familiar with the terrain, to decide on the best approach to each fence, and to note the bends of the course and the distances marked on the rails, so as not to waste a

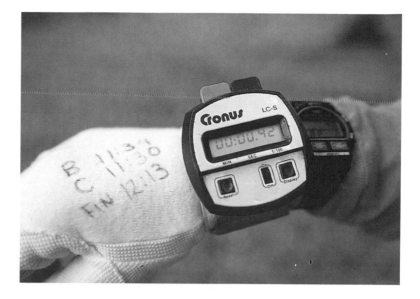

An easily readable stopwatch is essential for all the endurance phases. Minimum times can be noted on the back of your hand, or on a piece of paper in a plastic bag (to keep it waterproof) secured by tape to the forearm.

single metre. Every second counts. It is very important to pace the course at your normal walking stride and learn at what time to the minute you must arrive at each one of the various marks. For this purpose it is absolutely essential to wear an easily readable stop watch on your wrist that will enable you to check on the speed while galloping.

If starting times allow, try to watch a few riders on the course in order to verify your own calculations and to judge once again the conditions of the going. Pacing the course on foot also enables you to confirm your length of stride. This is essential knowledge for the purpose of measuring distances over the various parts of the cross-country course.

While a small measure of inaccuracy does not matter terribly during the roads and tracks phase, on the steeplechase course every second lost will significantly affect the final placing; on the other hand, too fast a time may tire the horse unnecessarily.

The Second Examination of the Cross-country Course

It is necessary to walk the cross-country course a second time to study it more thoroughly. On this occasion, walk alone or with only one knowledgeable companion. Every single obstacle must be measured, distances between the elements of combinations

The second walking of the cross-country course allows you to measure the obstacles.

must be carefully paced, alternatives assessed, and an ideal line decided upon, which will depend on how well you know the horse and on the final placing aimed for in the particular event.

Do not be too proud to use a yardstick to check on your evaluation of the height and breadth of obstacles, the depth of water, or the distances between elements of difficult combinations. Depending on the take-off point, an obstacle may measure 0.85 cm or 1.05 m; the human eye is easily deceived. An oxer may appear to be 1.45 m wide, when it actually measures 1.65 m. Depending on the type of obstacle and the ground conditions, a distance of 3.4 m between the elements of an obstacle would demand that it be negotiated as a bounce while if the distance were 3.8 m putting in an extra canter stride would be preferable.

On an unfamiliar course, I find it most difficult to decide on the right number of strides between the elements of combinations. So much depends on the sloping of the ground, the ground conditions, and the horse's speed and style of jumping. It is always advisable to obtain the opinions of fellow competitors and, if possible, to watch other competitors tackling a special difficulty. For example, a tree trunk positioned 4.20 m from the far edge of the water may, depending on the depth of the water and the height of the log, involve a bounce, one canter stride or, exceptionally and at the cost of tiring effort, two canter strides. I do not hold with the often heard comment: 'I am not going to worry about this problem before the time has come for my horse and me to face it'. All top international riders, be they show-jumpers or eventers, know precisely how they are going to approach every obstacle and avoid leaving things to chance. The art consists of being sufficiently flexible to be able to depart at the last moment from the predetermined plan if circumstances require. Flexibility does not invalidate the necessity of deciding on a detailed strategy; the greater the success of the strategy, the sooner one acquires the considerable degree of experience needed to change a plan at the final critical moment.

Deciding on the Ideal Line

Once you have decided on the precise take-off point and angle of approach for each individual obstacle, you must then consider the best line to follow over distances of 20 to 100 m between obstacles. This will depend on the stage of proficiency of the horse, the speed determined and the ground conditions. In optimum conditions, the ideal line would be the one that a racing driver would choose. To engrave this line in my mind, I note some landmarks between the fences such as tufts of grass, stones, twigs or posts, etc. I also frequently thus mark possible shortcuts. You must however beware of being led astray by the marks made by colleagues and also bear in mind that some of those personal landmarks may have suddenly vanished at the time of riding the course.

Shortcuts can save time but may involve some risks. Their

Riding your personal ideal line. Make a mental note of the natural features, such as bushes or tufts of grass, which mark the line of approach to each fence.

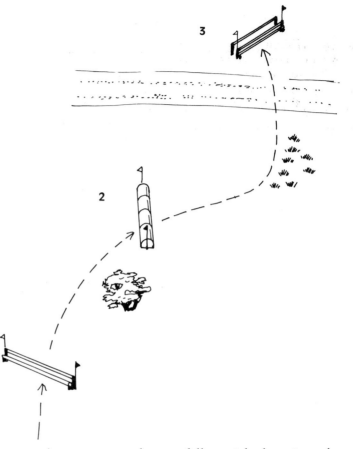

time-saving advantage must be carefully weighed against the possibility of difficult going.

Dividing the Course into Timed Sections

I have also got into the habit of dividing the course into sections timed in minutes. You must first find out the times that have been ridden on previous occasions or that appear possible, then, depending on the horse you will be riding, and, having made a realistic appraisal of all circumstances, you can establish your personal timing plan. Assuming a total time of ten minutes, mentally divide the course into ten sections of 60 seconds which means that you must look at your watch ten times en route to compare your actual time with the predetermined one. The art is to make a realistic estimation of the possible speed over a particular part of the course which may perhaps include a steep slope, a 180 degree turn or a water combination. Depending on circumstances, over a one-minute section, the average speed can be between 450 m per minute or almost 700 m per minute. In this matter you can only call on experience and considerable practice. At the Luhmuhlen national championship in June 1985 (the first time I participated in that event and therefore the course was new to me), I had set myself a minimum time of nine minutes. On the basis of the subdivision of the course into periods of so many minutes, I managed to achieve a time of 9.01 minutes, which was in fact the fastest time.

In the next event, the international three-day event at Achselschwang in September 1985 – my second start at this venue – I set myself a minimum time of ten minutes and managed to complete the course in 10.04 minutes, the third fastest time on the day.

The interesting thing about the 1986 event at Achselschwang is that the fastest times were achieved by two riders who lived in the district and were therefore better acquainted with the course than riders from other localities. This confirms what all car drivers as well as riders know well, that you always make better time, with less wear and tear, on a road over which you travel very frequently. Corners are rounded and the ideal line is much more easily planned the third time than it is the first time.

It is important to reckon on about 5 per cent more time over each one-minute section than the optimum time in which you hope to be able to ride it. At Achselschwang, where the optimum time for completion of the course was ten minutes, I had allowed one minute thirty seconds for each section and, as already mentioned, I finished in 10.04 minutes.

What is the point of this division of the course into timed sections? The big advantage is that at any moment when riding the course you will be able to know with some measure of certainty how your time compares with the optimum time. Psychologically, this is of considerable benefit; it helps you to ride more calmly. In addition – other circumstances allowing – you can take an upward gradient more slowly, thereby saving the horse's energy, if you are within the projected time or, on the other hand, make up for lost time by galloping faster than normally on a downward gradient.

Measuring the ideal line on foot and dividing it into timed sections of one minute. This is a section of the 1985 Achselschwang course.

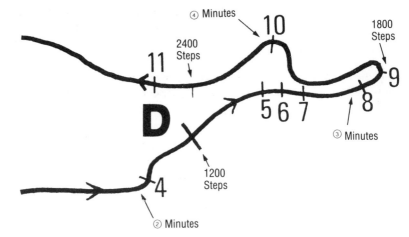

A further advantage is that you can plan in advance where to slow the speed to let the horse recuperate some energy, over a long upward gradient, for example, or where to ask it to speed on if the going is good, on the flat or downhill, for example.

Final Analysis of the Course: Running Through Your Notes

Walking the course a third time is enough if you have ridden over it already and know it fairly well. Over new terrain or in the case of a very important event, I maintain that it is absolutely necessary to make a fourth examination.

The last examination of the course is made early on the morning of the cross-country phase. This time you must walk the course absolutely alone, conscientiously running through the notes made while walking the course the first and second time, and coming to any final decision that remains to be made. Talking to fellow competitors and mulling over first impressions overnight may have made you think differently about some particular obstacle. Then there are other factors to take into consideration; it may have rained during the night, or, you may have walked the course the previous evening and conditions of visibility would be different if starting on the course around noon. I walk exactly along the ideal line I had figured out previously, make another mental note of my markers, grass tufts, bushes, twigs, etc., check again on the practicality of the plan-ned shortcuts – and thoroughly rehearse my timing programme.

| Tip 15 |

The various sections of the course should be walked at least four times in the case of major events and three times at least in the case of less important ones.

Above all, I savour the intense pleasure of being alone and at peace in the country at first light.

Observing the Opposition

Time permitting, you should watch as many competitors as possible at particularly difficult obstacles. A rider competing for the first time at Kloppenheim and observing how easily another competitor negotiates the big drop fence will be able to approach this formidable-looking obstacle with greater peace of mind.

I have frequently altered my carefully rehearsed plan at the last moment as a result of such observations. At Achselschwang there was a nasty pheasant feeder set at an angle just about 9–11 m after a jump into a sunken road. I had decided to ride very prudently and had allowed for three cantering strides between the two elements. However, before starting myself, I had seen another competitor do it easily in two strides, which is what I did thus enabling me to ride faster and take a shorter route.

I have often seen horses flounder suddenly in what appeared to be shallow water because they found a previously undetectable hole in the bottom. I would then approach the water even more cautiously than usual, or, alternatively, I would avoid the hazard by going well to the left or the right.

Conclusion

The importance of careful analysis of a course and of minute planning cannot be exaggerated. The cross-country phase of a three-day event usually has the greatest influence on the final placing; besides which it is the only phase that can be so thoroughly planned.

Seeking advice from fellow competitors and experts, repeatedly walking the course, establishing a time schedule for each part of the course, these are all the ingredients of the plan. It is however essential to be able to react instinctively and appropriately to changed circumstances. Unexpectedly heavy going, unaccountable tiredness of the horse are things that cannot be foreseen and taken into account, but it is precisely in such circumstances that careful planning comes to the rescue. It enhances concentration, it makes for safe riding and thereby for coolness which is the best condition for correct reaction at the critical moment.

CHAPTER 4 The Dressage Test

The Ever Increasing Importance of Dressage

At the Los Angeles Olympic Games in 1984, amongst about fifty participants in the three-day event, the gold medallist was one of the seven best placed at the end of the dressage phase. The first ten placed in the whole event, with one exception, were placed amongst the best half in the dressage phase, six of them coming in the first third. The same thing happened at the World Championship at Luhmuhlen in 1982 and at Gawler in Australia in 1986.

Being placed in the last third in the dressage deprives you of any chance of a good placing in all three-day events of any consequence. This is why I consider that the dressage aptitude of a prospective three-day eventer is far more important than its jumping ability or jumping style; relative jumping ability can be polished by patience and muscular fitness; but nervousness or a deficient knee action, for example, will remain lasting handicaps for dressage.

The dressage has become much more important in recent years because the performances of all the top riders and horses in the cross-country and showjumping phases have become equally impressive. In Los Angeles, two of the medallists finished without faults in either the cross-country or the showjumping. The first ten had either insignificant or no time penalties and no refusals in the cross-country and no faults in the showjumping. Altogether there were only four falls.

It is nearly always the dressage results that tip the scales. Horses that perform well in the dressage are usually well placed at the conclusion of the event. It is evident, therefore, that being on the bit, obedient to the legs, and ready to lengthen or shorten the stride smoothly, are factors that in the course of the last few years have also become more important for the cross-country. The height and breadth of the obstacles has not increased much, but combinations have become trickier and have frequently involved turns of 90 to 180 degrees. Having a horse that stays

| Tip 16 |

When selecting a horse as a potential eventer consider carefully also his aptitude for dressage.

willingly on the bit is a great advantage in terms of time saved and economy of rider effort.

Preparation for the Dressage Test

The day before

To complete a three-day event the horse has to be as fit as possible: fitness implies stamina, eagerness, quick reaction, self-confidence and courage. As regards the dressage, this means settling and relaxing the horse, because the first essential is perfect calmness. Nerves and temperament have to be soothed. In my experience, it is not fully understood how much eventers can become apprehensive and overstrung in the dressage arena. Dressage may not be their strong point although the ability to respond quickly and effectively is probably the secret of their success on the cross-country course.

Preparation for the dressage test must start the day before at the latest, or preferably sooner. I show the horse the arena and its surroundings, and practise only suppling exercises for about an hour. I avoid conflict with the horse and overcorrection when problems arise, but he must be responsive. Finally, it is important to return the horse to his stable in a peaceful state of mind.

On the day of the test

For a long time I have taken to heart the advice and experiences set out in the books of Horst Karsten, Karl Schultz and Lucinda Green. Better three hours of riding than one minute too little. This does not of course mean relentless riding, but perhaps an hour's hacking in the early morning with some cantering, dismounting for a while, resting; undemanding suppling work; another rest; dressage-like work; another rest, then the final preparation before entering the arena.

Those frequent moments of respite are most important. Reiner Klimke also says that frequent interruptions of work, a return to the stable or allowing the horse to stand about unmounted are more beneficial than a thousand figures of the manege. Karl Schultz tells us how he would do about three to four hours preparation with his horse Madrigal, then rest near the arena for thirty minutes. After that time Madrigal would be poised, and even bored, and usually give a highly satisfactory performance.

What is the point of this long preparation? The idea is that the

| Tip 17 |

Allow two to four hours on the day for preparation of the dressage test.

horse must have become so relaxed, even to the extent of boredom, that glittering markers, brightly coloured flower tubs, umbrellas or the sight of other horses cannot shake his composure. Yet the horse must go forward fluently on the lightest possible contact, remain on the aids at the halt, and engage his hocks so as to produce smooth lengthening or shortening of the strides. In short the horse must give a presentation that is perfectly correct and also animated. The relaxation procedure has to achieve the right balance between slackness and tension which admittedly is not easy. Still experience has proved that a good dressage presentation in a three-day event depends principally on devoting ample time to the business of suppling, relaxing and thoroughly calming the horse.

Performing the Dressage Test

So many textbooks and articles have been written by dressage experts explaining how a rider must prepare himself and his horse in order to make a good impression on the dressage judges that I will limit my comments to a few remarks relevant to the present state of dressage in the three-day event, especially in the novice and intermediate events.

To start with, horse and rider must be perfectly groomed; the horse, as well as the rider's boots, must shine. The rider's clothes must be as clean and tidy as the horse's coat and mane. Dressage, after all, should be aesthetically pleasing. Since the dressage phase is becoming more of a decisive factor in modern eventing, a greater degree of formality in dress seems to be expected.

The first time I competed at Achselschwang in 1983 out of 60 riders I was one of the few to wear an ordinary black riding jacket for the dressage test. All the others wore the modern Olympic dressage version of the frock coat, although this particular event was just of medium standard. In 1985, at Achselschwang again, I rode the dressage test in a borrowed frock coat and was placed amongst the first third – same venue, same test, same horse – whereas in 1983 I trailed towards the end.

In the future, the rules regarding dress will probably depend on whether the dressage phase is going to assume an even greater importance than it has already. It is possible to imagine an even more decorative and fanciful uniform than the regulation 'tails' spread over the horse's croup; perhaps a special make-up and

Turnout and style are decisive factors of success in the dressage test.

pearl-strewn hair would appeal to the aesthetic sense of some judges.

The first movements in the test

With regard to the first movements of the test, there is a saying that must always be borne in mind: the first impression is all important. If a mark of 6, 7 or 8 is applied to 'entrance, halt, immobility and ride on', the next three movements will probably be marked in the same way, unless some gross fault is committed. The rider can count on the unanimous indulgence of the judges. Conversely he will have to overcome their prejudice if he flunks his entrance. If the horse waivers from the straight, comes to a crooked halt or does not stand still during the halt and then moves on hesitantly, the rider may have to put up with a mark of 5, 4, 3 or less. He will already have been branded for the next movements. The judges will have been instantly programmed to expect a faulty, imprecise, irregular presentation. Therefore,

Tip 18

Frequently rehearse Entrance, Halt, Salute, and Ride on. The first impression is most influential.

'enter, halt, salute and proceed' will have to be rehearsed many times. The rider must ask an assistant to observe him from the same position as a judge at C and criticise him mercilessly. Resolute forward movement is more likely to produce a straight entrance than hesitation. Although the position of the judges makes it difficult for them to appraise exactly the speed of the gait, it makes the slightest wavering from the centre line obvious.

The halt

The one movement that has to be performed repeatedly in the test is the halt. It is worth practising it with more patience and punctiliousness than any other. The three essential things for the halt are that the horse must stand completely still, remain on the bit and stand square; the most important being stillness. Teaching a horse to stand still must form part of every training session, and is a lesson that has to be practised in any location, in

The halt. A correct halt has to be practised with enormous patience and perseverance; it is the one movement that has to be performed repeatedly in the test, and will, therefore, reflect the overall marks.

open country or anywhere in a course of obstacles. Each time the horse must be required to stand still for at least ten seconds. A spoken admonition, a whisper, or a hiss are aids that can be used to good effect. Every event horse should also be taught to remain on the aids at the halt. Being very slightly behind the bit is judged more leniently than being above the bit. If the horse is even a little above the bit, the judges will deem – quite rightly – that the horse is agitated, resistant or disobedient.

The frequent repetition of the halt will prove the necessity of devoting sufficient time to relaxing the horse. If he is not perfectly relaxed and calm he will always be annoyed by the rider's repeated demands for a correct halt in the test.

Getting the horse to stand square is the most difficult thing. A halt with well engaged hocks can be achieved only by a horse that can flex the haunches. But suppleness of the haunches demands a superior degree of flexibility (Durchlassighkeit) that is not easily obtainable from the type of horse best suited to eventing.

However with the help of both the rein and leg aids we can prevent the horse from turning out the right or left hind as we halt before the judges; this simple obedience has to be obtained by training at home.

Correct manege figures
Precision in the execution of the required test movements depends on the skill of the rider rather than on the aptitudes of the horse. In this respect Josef Neckermann was outstandingly successful. He trained about twenty horses to Grand Prix level, and his precision always earned him high marks.

How can we gain or lose marks for those movements with our event horses? The critical movements are the serpentines, circles and the half-pass. In the serpentines for example it is not often that the loops are of equal dimensions with the horse correctly bent. To visualise their correct execution one should first draw them on paper; then trace them on foot in the manege, especially those at counter-canter.

Circles are seldom really circular; they are only too often egg or potato shaped. They also have to be drawn first on paper, marking the touching points, to help you to realise that it is impossible to ride a circle correctly if you go into the corners of the manege. Correctly executed conventional manege figures are the outward signs of concentration and precision in your work at home. Messing them up in the dressage test shows a lack of application by the rider.

Extensions

Regularity of gait at the extended trot, canter and walk is another nerve-racking thing, but a real test of impulsion, being on the bit, and submission. In general, the medium and extended trot are too hurried, but the extended canter, on the other hand, is too cautious. There is a kind of mystique about the medium trot; time after time it is demanded in the manege, as if it were the sole mark of a horse – or a rider – with a special talent for dressage. It is precisely because of this obsession that the medium and extended trot are so often criticised by the judges as being 'running' or 'hurried'.

I therefore advise riders to remain on the cautious side when they practise extended trot, contenting themselves with rather less than the horse is perhaps capable of doing. If the rider does not agitate the horse with unnecessary activity of seat and legs, he is more likely to relax and allow his impulsion to produce ground-covering strides.

It is better to curb your ambition than to risk hurry which is very likely to produce irregular strides. It is my experience that judges are less severe in marking a middle trot that lacks sufficient scope than one that is hurried, even though they may remark that it was 'insufficient'.

The extended canter does not cause as great a degree of difficulty. Inclining the trunk very slightly forward, closing the legs and advancing the arms is usually all that is needed to obtain the desired lengthening of the strides, as Reiner Klimke has so often demonstrated. Yet once more, I must repeat my advice to err on the side of caution rather than dare too much. I took too great a risk in my first extended canter with Akki in 1983 at Achselschwang – Akki changed behind just before we got to the opposite track. I got a mark of 1 from all three judges though the extension, in the opinion of probably 80 per cent of the spectators, deserved at least a 7. I am not questioning the judges' verdict; in the circumstances I would have marked this extension down as they did, but this demonstrates how much the slightest

| Tip 19 |

In extended trot, the more quietly you ride, the greater your chances of producing impressively ground-covering strides.

extension blunder can cost. If I have the slightest doubt about the ability and composure of the horse, I feel that it is better to be safe than sorry.

To ride forward or with caution?

Obviously impulsion is an essential element of dressage presentation, but with a horse that I do not entirely trust should I choose to obtain as much impulsion as possible or content myself with something rather less than enough? Judges must of course sift the wheat from the chaff. Irregularity and hurrying are mistakes which are sure to put you in the bottom third of the placings; a correct test with a horse properly on the bit and showing a lot of impulsion will earn high marks and a position amongst the first third. The rest of the field will lie somewhere in between with an average mark of around 5.5; an acceptable mark for a horse with an average dressage ability who is ridden cautiously. Caution is a policy that at least guards against accusations of 'hurrying', 'irregular' and 'off the aids'.

There is another good reason for caution in the development of impulsion. As the standard in eventing gets higher, dressage is more and more the phase that is going to tip the scale. The talented and correctly schooled dressage horses will dominate the field in this phase. It comes as no surprise to find Otto Ammerman doing so well in medium dressage with his brilliant Volturno after the latter was retired from the eventing scene. Inevitably the horses that the judges will place in the top quarter will be those that have performed well in normal dressage competitions at elementary or medium level. To my mind, this means that it is no longer possible to be placed at the top in the dressage phase with a horse that goes in the sort of outline that is good enough for pleasurable hacking.

Gone are the days when a rider could regard the hated dressage with a certain degree of contempt, knowing that the brilliance of his horse across country would always ensure him a top place at the end of a three-day event.

As the judges are treated to increasingly good dressage tests in the three-day event, they will invariably expect event horses to show the degree of collection, elevation and flexion of the haunches normally required of specialist dressage horses. It is a situation with which the riders will have to contend.

Tip 20

We have to accept that the standard of dressage in the three-day event is being raised continually.

Practical Advice About the Dressage

1. It can be deduced from what has been said that the eventing competitor should compete frequently in novice and elementary dressage tests and not only with young inexperienced horses.

2. Practise movements 1, 2 and 3 as often as the other movements but avoid doing them always at the same place or in the same surroundings. Horses quickly learn to anticipate the rider and in transitions to canter, for example, often become tense when they know what to expect.

3. Dressage training does not always have to be done in the manege. As Reiner Klimke said twenty years ago in his book *Military* (published in English in 1984 by J. A. Allen & Co., entitled *Horse Trials*), it is important to practise the movements in open country as well.

4. The flying change is not demanded in eventing and in the serpentine the horse must canter alternately with inside and outside lead. I have, therefore, never asked for, or allowed, a change of lead when training my horses for eventing.

5. Dressage is an exercise in concentration and application. Even the least talented partnership can achieve honourable results in the dressage through conscientious regular practise of dressage work. There is no other phase of eventing that can benefit more from concentrated study than the dressage.

As often as possible you should ask an expert to observe your work, give advice and correct errors.

Do not neglect to improve your seat by riding without stirrups. In this respect, occasionally riding an accomplished dressage horse can be very beneficial.

Finally, attend as many clinics as possible.

CHAPTER 5 The Veterinary Inspection and the Roads and Tracks

All horses taking part in horse trials have to undergo a veterinary inspection before the dressage and again before the showjumping. In a three-day event there is another inspection after the second stretch of roads and tracks.

It is the rider himself who has to run up the horse for the veterinary inspection before the dressage and showjumping and he should be properly attired though not in formal riding clothes. The horse should be well groomed, his hooves shining. He must be led in an ordinary snaffle. At the major events the display is interesting, because breeders and competitors can compare the horses, but the real purpose of the veterinary inspection is to protect the good name of the sport.

| Tip 21 |
It is not only to please the judges that horse and rider should be turned out as well as possible for the veterinary inspection.

Preparation

Everyone, young and old, should do some warming up exercises when they get out of bed in the morning, and horses must be allowed to limber up before the veterinary inspection. Banish the thought that this is to conceal some sort of lameness. Any kind of manipulation before the inspection must be strongly discouraged. Not only would it put the horse at considerable risk; it would also bring the sport into disrepute.

Cross-country Equipment for Horse and Rider

The rider wears leather boots and breeches; breeches with leather reinforcement give greater adherence to the saddle, and I always dampen the leather well before I get on the horse. Weather conditions will dictate what kind of upper-body clothing to wear, but it must allow complete freedom of movement. Gloves are advisable; they allow a better grip of the reins and a more sensitive contact with the horse's mouth. In very rainy weather, a spare pair ought to be carried or left in the ten minute box to change into before the start of the cross-country. A riding whip is of course an indispensable piece of equipment. I always

The veterinary inspection is an opportunity to compare the horses. It also puts the sport in a favourable light because it demonstrates concern for the horses' welfare.

pass my hand through the loop and have had loops stitched on to all my whips in such a manner that I can be certain that I will not drop the whip in any situation. I would not think either of riding the cross-country without spurs. There are strict rules regarding the design of the spurs; they must be blunt and of a maximum length of 2.5 cm. I have no experience of back protectors but I think that they are a good idea. The majority of riders now wear them and they will probably become obligatory in the near future.

The saddle used for cross-country is usually the jumping saddle worn in training. However in the major events, when the combined weight of rider and saddle has to be 75 kg, weights may

It is important that the rider is as well turned-out as the horse when running him up for the judges.

have to be carried. As for the reins, I prefer the 'English' rubber-covered reins to the 'German' webbing ones with martingale stops; they allow more precise adjustment. Opinions are divided on the subject of martingales; I am against them and have never used one even for showjumping. A martingale prevents or, at least, restricts the movement of the horse's neck – that fifth leg of the animal that is so important to the preservation of balance in precarious situations. The bit must also be of the same type as that used during training. With Akki Bua, however, I used a jointed snaffle when competing but a rubber snaffle during training. Strong pullers may be easier to control with a Pelham. The horse must be equipped with overreach boots in front and brushing boots both in front and behind; they should also be worn for training. Exercise bandages are an alternative to brushing boots, but this is a matter of preference. Studs are always advisable; it is better to be over cautious by fitting larger studs than none at all. It is too late to regret your negligence when the horse skids in a turn on a slippery patch of grass.

Recently it has become common practice at the big events to smear thickly the horse's fore and hind legs with Vaseline or some other kind of grease which is a good idea. It can often prevent a fall or an injury if the horse grazes an obstacle with his legs.

Counting the Horse's Pulse

In the three-day event, the horse has to be trotted up before a vet after the second roads and tracks. If the horse's pulse rate has not yet returned to normal, it will be examined again a few minutes later. As stated earlier concerning interval training, a rider ought to know his horse's normal pulse rate. As the vet takes the horse's pulse, the rider should stand close enough to him to hear him counting. It is the only way of knowing whether the horse has recovered sufficiently after the second roads and tracks. If the pulse rate is above 100, it should be taken again five to seven minutes later. Should it then still be above 80, it is doubtful that the cross-country course can be completed at the speed contemplated.

The Roads and Tracks

The point of the first roads and tracks is to limber up the horse in preparation for the cross-country or, at the big events, the gruelling steeplechase. Ideally one should be able to give the horse a short sharp canter as a pipe-opener, but unfortunately this is rarely possible. The second roads and tracks is intended to allow the horse to recover from the exertion of the steeplechase and the rider must think only of preserving the strength of the horse as much as possible.

The Start of the First Roads and Tracks

Akki Bua would always be so keyed up before the start that it could take more than one assistant to hold him while I mounted. My stirrup leathers would already have been shortened because the horse's excitement would have made it impossible to shorten them later. To spare his nerves, I would mount no sooner than about one minute before the start.

Horse and rider are equipped for the roads and tracks exactly as for the steeplechase or the cross-country. There is no need to add or dispense with any piece of equipment (spurs, whip, breastplate, martingale, etc.) as the risk of finding oneself ill-equipped to cope with an unpredictable difficulty on the roads and tracks is too great.

The rider should take the start in as relaxed a frame of mind as possible. It is not as if every second counted but it is at last the beginning of an event which has taken such a long – and hopefully enjoyable – time to prepare.

The route will have been committed to memory like a piece of poetry, especially the obligatory check points. One must ride every section at the speed and gait planned when studying the course while aiming for a slightly higher speed, for example 240 rather than 220m per minute, in order to allow the horse a somewhat longer recovery pause before the start of the next phase.

The Second Roads and Tracks

With the second roads and tracks, the aim should be to cover it in as short a time as possible without tiring the horse too much. You can let him go downhill at an easy canter, unless the ground slopes too steeply. Conversely the least exacting gait is used when going uphill.

I ride the second part of the roads and tracks on an almost loose rein, allowing the horse to go in a long outline, thus

44

<table>
<tr><td>

Tip 22

Remember that the aim of the first part of the roads and tracks is to loosen and limber up the horse; in the second part you must aim at allowing the horse to recover completely from the effect of exertion on the steeplechase course before starting on the cross-country.

</td></tr>
</table>

sparing it unnecessary effort. Experience has taught me that a quiet canter is less tiring than a trot of the same speed and I ride as in interval training with fairly long periods of cantering interspersed with two or three minutes of walking. For example, if the second roads and tracks is 6 km long, I may ride the first 800 m after the steeplechase at canter or a brisk trot to take advantage of the speed gained over the steeplechase course, then walk for five minutes (80 m per minute), canter (380 m per minute), three minutes walk, five minutes canter, three minutes walk, one minute canter. If we can cover the distance at an average speed of 240 m per minute, it allows the horse an extra two and half minutes to recover.

Summary

For the roads and tracks, the three rules are:

1. Remember the situation of the compulsory turning flags.
2. Remember that the purpose of the first part is to limber up the horse.
3. Remember to give the horse ample opportunity to recover from exertion between the steeplechase and the cross-country.

The roads and tracks will then be what they are intended to be; the least stressful phase of the whole competition: nothing more than a relaxing hack.

CHAPTER 6   The Steeplechase

This is the phase that I most look forward to, it is what nature designed the horse for; to extend himself freely at a gallop, to fly over obstacles. It is exhilarating for the rider as well. Achieving the optimum time is a matter of seat, regulation of speed, approach to the fences and working out the shortest route.

Yet the steeplechase is for many riders the most daunting phase of the event. The following tips may reassure them that with time and experience they will come to enjoy it instead of feeling apprehensive about it.

The Seat

When studying the racing seat, we cannot do better than observe professional steeplechase jockeys, especially in events such as the famous Grand National with its difficult and varied obstacles. The stirrup leathers should be from six to ten holes shorter than for dressage and shorter perhaps than for the cross-country but still must enable one to stay as close to the saddle as possible and to use seat and leg aids energetically if one feels the horse hesitating before an obstacle. I therefore ride eight holes shorter in the steeplechase, cross-country and showjumping than for dressage. Thus, between the fences I can stay balanced on the stirrups like a jockey. It is always advisable to support both hands on the horse's neck, holding both reins in one hand and linking the hands by making a so-called bridge with the reins above the horse's neck to help balance the rider and therefore the horse. Although, as I have just said, there are occasions when one may have to sit in order to urge the horse on at a jump, it must be realised that in general the 'heavy' seat makes excessive demands on the horse's strength and costs precious seconds.

The racing and cross-country seats are not the same as the showjumping seat. The showjumping seat must allow the rider to drive and yet enable him to accompany the horse over the obstacles with great suppleness, advancing his hands and his

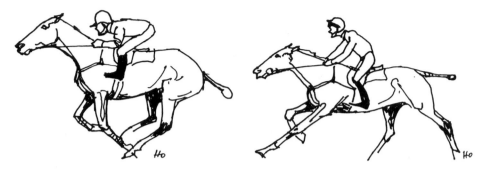

The stirrups should be as short as possible. Balanced on the stirrups, the rider must keep his centre of gravity as close to the saddle as possible: left, correct; right, incorrect.

upper body considerably to preserve contact with the horse's mouth. This is the seat advocated by Caprilli before the First World War. On the steeplechase course and across country, the motto is, safety first. That is, safety of the horse at the moment of landing. The higher the speed over the jump, the more the forehand of the horse should be lightened, allowing instantaneous resumption of speed after the jump. It is for this reason that steeplechase jockeys sit behind the movement during the jump with stirrups pushed forward. On the other hand, Lucinda Green has developed an exemplary eventing seat. She still sits lightly over the biggest obstacles, remaining very close to the saddle and keeps her legs at the girth or only slightly in front of the vertical. This allows her to:

— React instantaneously in tricky situations.
— Keep her seat when a horse refuses.
— Ride fast, even in turns.
— And, most importantly, it reduces the risk of her horse coming 'off the legs' (disengaging its hindquarters).

It is important to develop the steeplechase seat in order to be able to maintain it over fences. The hands must then, of course, advance to give the horse complete freedom to use his neck, but not his trunk. In showjumping the rider's knee is the pivot which allows a considerable forward displacement of the upper body, but in steeplechasing the rider must remain balanced on the stirrups; jockeys cannot grip with their knees.

Tip 23

In steeplechasing, the rider's seat must remain close to the saddle over the fences. Only the hands are advanced.

Regulation of the Speed

Riders are often advised to hold back somewhat on the first circuit of the course. I do not agree totally with that. The horse

The rider's seat during the jump: top, incorrect; below, correct.

must, of course, be allowed to find his legs after the start but I can see no reason for preventing him from developing his best speed after the first 100 m. It is over the first circuit that the horse feels fresher and more capable of maximum speed. Even in the 100 m race, maximum speed is attained over the first 50 m (apart from the sprint to the finish). In trotting racing, the overall speed plays as important a role as the final sprint to the winning post. To maintain a good average speed, the trotter must be allowed to develop its greatest speed over the first half of the race. It is in accordance with this principle that I always develop the greatest speed over the first circuit of the course. I can then allow the horse to gallop in a somewhat more restrained fashion over the second circuit. It is however extremely important to check your watch frequently to make sure that you are well within the time decided on.

Allowing the horse to develop full speed over the first circuit does in fact save energy. The speed can then be reduced over the second circuit. The opposite policy necessitates a burst of speed at the end which takes a lot more out of the horse.

What if the going is heavy? Should I deliberately renounce my plan to finish in the optimum time so as to preserve the horse's strength for the cross-country? The answer is that I ride as fast as the going permits. Amongst thoroughbreds, there are hard- and

| Tip 24 |

Attain maximum speed as soon as possible. The speed can then be slowed towards the end, giving the horse more time to recover.

soft-going specialists, but I stick to my original plan unless I feel that the horse is losing heart, then I give it up. There is a 30 to 40 minute interval between the steeplechase and the cross-country and a well-trained horse of a suitable type should be able to recover completely from exertion during that time.

Steeplechase obstacles are more imposing than hurdles but they are not show-jumps either. It is impossible to give a precise indication of their maximum dimension. They must be treated with respect, but, unlike showjumping, it is not necessary to worry about dislodging a pole by jumping too flat. A steeplechase fence must be flown over in a fluent manner. Never think of slowing down, collecting or checking the horse; it would all waste too much time.

Steeplechase fences must not be jumped as show-jumps; the trajectory must be long and low: a) incorrect, b) correct.

a

b

The lower the trajectory over a steeplechase fence, the less time is wasted.

I start to drive on about 50 m before the fence. The gallop strides must become longer and more resolute. This driving on soon convinces horses that they can easily clear the obstacle ahead. A flat trajectory of 6 m is better than a high one of 4 m.

It is especially in the approach to the first fences that you must drive energetically, with the additional use of voice and whip if necessary. They are probably the first obstacles that the horse will have been asked to tackle on the day and he must pay attention. From a distance they do not seem to be monstrous but because of the speed of approach they suddenly loom menacingly and, understandably, many horses will try to run out to one side or the other.

The next fences should be plain sailing; the horse is alert and has warmed to the task, and the rider need not use such emphatic aids.

The last fences, however, will probably require greater concentration on the part of the rider. What are the horse's reserves of energy? Is the horse starting to drag his hind legs? The gallop may be starting to feel listless. It is towards the end of the course that stumbles or even falls are most likely. The tired horse may put in a short stride unexpectedly before take-off. The last fences must, therefore, be ridden at with care and on a firm contact. It may be necessary to execute a slight half-halt just before the fence to ensure a safe take-off point and to 'bend the bow' again before the jump.

A surprising number of steeplechase courses are laid out over sloping terrain. As I have already said: downhill – throttle out; uphill – steadily, but beware of fences built on a downward slope, many riders and horses tend to get too close before take-off.

Every Metre Counts

A distance of one metre corresponds to a tenth of a second; ten gallop strides take about five seconds. Which just shows how important it is to walk the course attentively and decide on the shortest route. If the starting box is wide, position yourself well to the left or the right, whichever side helps to shorten the way. Fences before or on a curve must of course be taken on the inside.

A skilled motorist will swing out a little before a tight turn, in order to be able to come out of it close to the inside verge. If the curvature of the bend is slight, he stays close to the inside before the change of direction so as to save as much time as possible. The same technique applies to race riding. Akki Bua is pronouncedly 'left-handed' on a racecourse. He is as supple as a cat when the track bends to the left and hugs the inside of the curve in as time-saving a manner as possible. Conversely, I have great difficulty keeping him to the inside if the bend is to the right; he always attempts to go wide.

All horses are either left- or right-handed, and we must take this into account when planning our strategy for the steeplechase.

Summary

Every tenth of a second counts on the racecourse. It is important to plan the shortest line and to aim at a low trajectory over fences. For the sake of safety, during the jump the steeplechase jockey advances his hands but not his upper body.

CHAPTER 7 The Cross-country

Before the Start

I always try to have a few minutes in hand at the end of the roads and tracks to give the horse a longer respite before the cross-country; that is from ten to twelve or thirteen minutes at the major events. This also gives more time to concentrate my thoughts on what is lying ahead.

First, the horse must be trotted up before the vet. His pulse will be taken a first time, and perhaps again seven minutes later, by which time it should have returned to below 80. Shoes have to be checked; the girth must be loosened; the horse must be offered a drink, have his nostrils wiped with a wet sponge, and then walked in hand. A rider will need at least two assistants.

Having entrusted the horse to their care, I can sit down alone for eight to twelve minutes in as quiet a place as I can find, rest my body and prepare myself mentally for the severity of the next phase. I have to be strictly alone because I must once again go 'through my lines': recalling every single obstacle, every turn, my personal markers, the obligatory turning flags and of course my timing programme. I consider the state of the ground and wonder whether I will be able to ride according to plan, and I find out the times of the riders who have preceded me.

Tip 26
Take advantage of the pause before the start of the cross-country to relax and to concentrate mentally on the task ahead. Go through your plan again as if reciting a piece of poetry.

The Start

All my horses have been very keyed up at the start and I have always needed a helper to lead us into the starting box. Once given the signal to start, I set off as briskly as possible on the shortest way to fence 1.

As over the steeplechase course, I take advantage of the horse's freshness to make good time and I allow the horse to develop a totally unrestrained fluent gallop. A fast start is of much greater advantage than a desperate race against time at the end. However at novice horse trials, where there are no roads and tracks, the horse must be given time to warm up before it can be asked to develop its best speed.

The First Fences

The same principles apply to the jumping of the first cross-country obstacles as in the steeplechase. The rider must drive on determinedly without checking the speed so that the horse realises that this is serious business. He should enjoy jumping those first obstacles and clearing them without having to be held back. Because of the speed, in a combination, 10.5 m between the elements may be too short a distance to allow for two strides and 5.5 m would probably have to be treated as a bounce.

The absolute opposite tactics apply to the jumping of the last fences. The horse's springs will have lost their elasticity, his frame will become more and more drawn out. He will try increasingly to put in a short stride before take-off; and, consequently, will need two strides for a 8.5 m combination.

Over the jump, the rider is already looking at the course ahead.

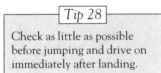

The rider will have to be far more attentive and active at this stage, and his reactions must be quicker. He must also listen carefully to his horse to ascertain how much the horse has in reserve and how much more effort he can demand fairly.

Fatigue may induce a refusal or cause the horse to straddle a fence, and many horses gallop feebly without gaining much ground. A sloppy stride causes them to jump carelessly, and often they are unable to respond quickly if they get into trouble.

The Approach to the Obstacles

Every half-halt costs time, as Reiner Klimke tells us; it is also a waste of the horse's energy. There are, of course, some obstacles where a perceptible or even a very firm checking of speed is necessary. Nevertheless, you must train yourself and the horse to tackle as many obstacles as possible in a flowing manner, though perhaps at a somewhat more restrained speed. It is rather like driving on a road with frequent S bends. After the tenth bend you drive faster, not because you use more petrol but because you brake gently and accelerate at the right places, thus negotiating the turns in a smooth manner.

Similarly over the cross-country course, I avoid braking suddenly and then 'chasing' the horse between the obstacles. Smooth driving makes for optimum speed.

Riding On After a Jump

One of the most important keys to a fast time is the horse going forward immediately and energetically after landing. It is only a slight exaggeration to say that this is what distinguishes the professional from the amateur. It is something that can be practised on home ground and on every possible occasion. It must become an ingrained habit for both horse and rider.

Tip 27

I can really push on over the first two thirds of the course. Over the last third, safety must be the prime consideration.

Tip 28

Check as little as possible before jumping and drive on immediately after landing.

CHAPTER 8 Jumping Parallels

Jumping a parallel in impeccable style.

Most obstacles of this type are easier to negotiate than they appear at first sight. Oxers, log stacks, milk churn stands, bench and table, pheasant coops, etc. will pose problems only to riders who approach them with exaggerated respect. Throw your heart over them! Go at them with impulsion, impulsion, and more

Approach a triple bar with lots of impulsion to take off as close as possible to the lowest bar. The same rule applies to the jumping of a log in front of a ditch.

impulsion. Oxers, which sometimes are made to look like small houses, seem to shrink when one measures them carefully. Even in the major three-day events they must not exceed 1.1 m in height or a breadth of 2 m. Now even a cow could clear a height of 1.4 m. As regards breadth, note that the normal galloping stride of a horse is 3.5 m and that on the racecourse a horse may cover in one stride a distance of 5 to 7 m when jumping over a fence or a ditch. Most of the parallels in a novice showjumping competition are bigger than those we find on a cross-country course for novice horses. The important thing is not to let yourself be overawed by the deceptively formidable appearance of such obstacles, especially of the newly built ones.

Ascending Parallels

Determined forward riding is obviously also the rule at ascending parallels. Horse and rider can help each other out if something goes wrong, by taking off early or putting in a short stride. This is the easiest type of obstacle for horses and it rarely causes a fall or a stumble.

True Parallels

| Tip 30 |

Ascending parallels and obstacles built on a downward slope present little difficulty, providing impulsion is maintained.

True parallels are more difficult. They require more attention on the part of the rider and experience on the part of the horse, who must have learnt to advance a foreleg quickly during landing. The horse must be perfectly on the aids. At a big oxer, it should be decidedly collected in the last strides of the approach, to bend it like a bow before shooting an arrow. The last strides before take-off should be short and bouncy. I never ride fast at a big true parallel; the horse could take off too soon and land on top of the

a

b

Jumping a true parallel: a) the horse's frame is too extended and consequently the forelegs are not sufficiently tucked under; b) 'bending the bow' before take-off, the horse can project himself over the jump with more power.

True parallels must be tackled with great care, especially those built on downward sloping terrain. They call for mental concentration and energetic riding to keep the horse constantly on the aids.

obstacle rather than on the other side. But what I particularly dread is that extra half-stride which can so easily cause a tumble. I take the same precautions when jumping or approaching at an oblique angle or cutting a corner. With all true parallels, by the seventh or eighth minute one must assess the horse's readiness to extend a foreleg quickly when landing and realise that jumping at an angle can transform a 1.6m spread into a 2.5m one.

Parallels on an Ascending Slope

A parallel built on an ascending slope must be approached with great determination. Galloping uphill frees the forehand and brings the hind legs well underneath the horse. This puts the horse positively on the aids, making it easier for the rider to drive on and find the best place for take-off, but jumping a parallel uphill safely requires considerable impulsion and fluency. If the rein contact is loose the horse will stop, realising that he has not enough impulsion to throw his own weight plus that of the rider safely over the jump.

The rider should start to drive 15 to 20m before the jump. Driving on for only one or two strides is usually insufficient.

Jumping a parallel uphill is a pleasant experience, rather like jumping an ascending oxer.

Jumping Downhill

All obstacles built on a descending slope are tricky and relatively dangerous. When galloping downhill, most horses will, given the chance, try to let themselves roll, throwing almost all the weight on the forehand, leaning on the hand, and consequently coming off the leg aids. If the rider allows this to happen, impulsion and control are lost. The horse may try to take off too soon and put in a half-stride; or he will get too close to the obstacle and find himself unable to get his forelegs over.

Distance is more difficult to estimate when galloping downhill; contours become blurred and the unevenness of the ground is more difficult to perceive. Stumbling on landing is the frequent consequence of a big jump on steeply descending gradients. You need to have rolled a heavy object down a hill only once to understand how awesome a force gravity is when unleashed.

It is in the second and third part of the cross-country phase that downhill jumping is particularly tricky. With increasing

All obstacles built on a descending slope have to be approached with care. Riders should beware of letting their horses 'roll along' as is often the tendency when galloping downhill.

fatigue, and especially when galloping downhill, the horse responds less promptly to the aids, starts to disengage its hind legs and to overload the forehand. Caution is, therefore, the word, whether approaching a parallel or an upright.

And so, when jumping downhill, speed and time are for me of least concern. I ride with concentration and special regard for safety, making sure that my horse stays on the aids. I did come to grief once, however, on heavy going, when Akki failed to lift his front end in good time.

Banking Obstacles

The banking of parallel-type obstacles is a serious problem. It is a necessary art which the horse has to master for there are some big oxers that could not be surmounted, or surmounted only with difficulty, if the horse did not bank them. But there is a danger; horses find out that banking those big obstacles spares effort, they become negligent, and expect to be able to do so everywhere with impunity. At the Munich Olympic Games I saw Mark Phillips fall when his horse tried to bank a brushwood oxer and, on another occasion, one of my horses ridden by a friend fell for the same reason at a loosely filled hay rack. There are not many obstacles that need banking in horse trials for novice or even intermediate horses (except of course walls and tables). At Fussgonheim there is a massive-looking pheasant coop, about 2.5 m wide, which is very solidly built and can therefore be safely banked. When I have used this course for training, I have sometimes banked this particular obstacle out of a trot.

I do train young horses to bank walls and earthworks forming

Successful banking. The rider, prepared for an unpleasant surprise, maintains contact with the horse's mouth and sits down firmly.

part of bounce combinations. When they have developed confidence in their rider and allow themselves to be driven at any obstacle, they quickly develop the right instinct and know when one has to be banked, but I never let them bank timber which can be jumped in one stride. There is too great a risk of teaching a horse to expect that every impressive looking obstacle is a really big one.

CHAPTER 9 Jumping Uprights

Uprights, in general, are easier then parallels, but can sometimes be trickier.

Even in major events they are never higher than 1.2 m in favourable conditions, a modest height for any fairly experienced partnership, but, because of this, horses and riders tend to treat them with insufficient respect. I have certainly experienced as

Jumping uprights: a) late take-off; b) too much speed in the approach and premature take-off; c) a perfect jump.

many stumbles and falls at inoffensive looking uprights as at parallels and the cause has always been that the horse has failed to tuck up his forelegs enough.

The speed over a cross-country course is much greater than in showjumping so that over the same distance the horse exerts itself far more. At a speed of 500 m per minute, if the horse gets even slightly under an obstacle he will need a lightning reaction of the forelegs to clear it. Not all event horses have a 'nimble' foreleg, many are designed for fast, time-saving, but often careless, skimming of obstacles. Experienced riders and horses approach particularly daunting looking obstacles with caution and respect; it is precisely because uprights appear innocuous that they are the cause of so many falls.

If there is a filling in front of a big upright, the fence becomes one of the most straightforward obstacles. With good going and even terrain, it can be approached without change of speed and jumped on a long, low trajectory. Even if the horse tries a half-stride before take off, the presence of this ground line helps to avoid a fall. Care is still needed in the approach to a relatively inoffensive looking obstacle if it is situated in the last third of the course, when the horse is running out of steam. In this case it is advisable to slow down and collect the horse. Here again, caution rather than speed is called for.

The Nimble Foreleg

Uprights without some filling at their base, such as pheasant feeders, gates, railings, tollgates, etc. must be approached with much more care; it is at these obstacles that a 'nimble' foreleg is essential. It is nearly always necessary to slow down because it is too risky to go for a long jump at unaltered speed. Many gates are painted white or striped and a railway crossing gate may be just one bar without any ground line. Horses are very liable to get 'under' them – with more dire consequences than at an ascending parallel; in such a situation a foreleg can never be nimble enough to get the horse out of trouble.

The greater the speed of approach, the more important it is to place the horse for a correct take-off. I do not belong to the company of those who believe that they can leave it to the horse to find the right take-off and that all that the rider has to do is drive on energetically. I am convinced that it is this attitude that

Tip 33

To negotiate an upright without a ground line, a correct take-off is essential.

is most frequently the cause of falls at uprights. The horse is intrepidly urged forwards as though approaching a parallel, a ditch or a Trakehner. At the last moment the horse hesitates, puts in a half-stride and horse and rider are in for a somersault.

Slanting Uprights

Uprights built on a slope so that the ground is lower at one end than at the other have never given me any trouble. When walking the course, one should look out for the best place to jump. This will depend on the ideal line, and also on the state of the going. Furthermore this sort of obstacle can measure 0.8 m at one extremity and 1.2 m at the other.

I have found out that horses are more attentive when galloping on the side of a hill; they are easier to keep on the aids than when galloping downhill or on even ground.

Uprights built across an uphill gradient are also straightforward. Here again great impulsion is the important thing. There are however two exceptions when extra care is called for. The first is an obstacle like a 0.6 m pheasant feeder or log pile on top of a small hill, at the end of a relatively steep climb, at which refusals are quite common. Horses are more or less out of breath and are taken by surprise, especially as they cannot see where they are going to land. They have to jump bravely into the unknown. Here one should ride energetically, on a short rein, and encourage the horse with legs, voice and whip.

The other exception is where the steeper the slope and the further the take-off, the bigger the jump. For example, an innocuous 90 cm pheasant feeder can represent a jump of 1.3 m. Akki hit just such an obstacle once and we very nearly came to grief. At the end of a fairly long climb, he was momentarily out of breath and did not tuck his forelegs under sufficiently quickly. When approaching an obstacle built on an upward gradient it is very important to consider the condition of the horse. At uprights particularly, the horse must still have enough strength to tuck his forelegs under nimbly.

Jumping uprights downhill is a different proposition altogether. You often, for example, have to jump downhill over a pheasant feeder or a gate into a road; it is the sort of obstacle for which I have the greatest respect. The right take-off is more difficult to estimate, and the forehand is more loaded, which makes it more difficult for the horse to tuck up its front feet. In those circumstances, I slow down, shorten the canter strides, and keeping a firm contact on the reins with my hands held high, I concentrate on a close take-off. The shortened reins with a firm contact help the horse to use his neck as a fifth leg and avoid a fall should he strike a rail. The more you shorten the strides, the closer you can get to the obstacles and there is less risk of the horse losing his balance if he does strike the rail with his forelegs. Furthermore this sort of approach is in accord with the horse's preservation instinct. When cantering uphill or, and especially, downhill, horses will instinctively avoid making a long jump.

Jumping Into or Out of Shade

Fences, such as pheasant feeders, posts and rails or gates are frequently built at the entrance or exit of a copse so that one has to jump from light to shade or vice versa.

Jumping into shade is not usually a difficulty; the obstacle is

Jumping into shade.

clearly visible to the horse in most cases. However, the technique does call for good impulsion and the rider should aim for a short jump and be prepared for a refusal at the last moment.

Jumping out of shade into light is much trickier; it is not easy to estimate distance and suitable take-off point. Although the obstacle is usually fairly straightforward, it should still be ridden at carefully, and the rider should aim for a short, tidy jump.

Jumping Uprights at an Angle

A big advantage of uprights is that you can, and indeed often must, jump them at an angle. All show-jumpers are conversant with the technique which can facilitate the jumping of a particular obstacle as well as saving time. Jumping at an angle increases the distance between the horse's forefeet and the top pole of the obstacle. In showjumping it diminishes the risk of a knock-down; on the cross-country course it diminishes the risk of a fall. The technique has to be practised on home ground time after time over small obstacles, not only to teach the horse to jump at an angle, but also to build up his confidence. However, we must distinguish between an approach perpendicular to the obstacle with a turn to the right or left at the last moment, and an oblique approach, at an angle of, say, 45 degrees, followed by a jump at the same angle.

Many obstacles on a cross-country course have to be jumped at an angle because of the contour of the ground. In addition the ground may sometimes be badly poached at the middle of the obstacle and still relatively firm on either side.

The time-saving advantage of jumping at an angle is obvious enough, and it is surprising that so many riders miss opportunities to do so and thus throw away invaluable seconds. It might do them good to do some showjumping against the clock. A rider who has carefully walked the course and planned the shortest possible route will find that about half the obstacles on a cross-country course can be jumped or approached obliquely.

While on the subject of uprights, I must stress how important it is to distinguish the jumping of uprights at the beginning of the course from those at the end. During the first half of the course, the horse is keen, alert, full of impulsion and vigour. One can usually expect him to stand off well and jump big. Even if he does get a little under an obstacle, he will be quick to tuck his forelegs

Tip 34

Approaching an obstacle, or jumping it at an angle, can often facilitate the jump as well as saving time. Rider and horse must train at home until they have perfected the technique.

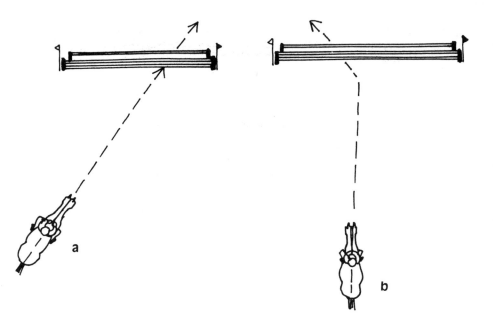

Jumping at an angle: the choice is a) taking the shortest route at an angle to the obstacle, or b) riding straight at the obstacle and jumping it at an angle, in order to land on the shortest line to the next obstacle.

under, and still have enough strength to jump acrobatically to get himself out of trouble. But strength and quickness diminish progressively from minute to minute, kilometre to kilometre. Increasingly the rider will have to help the horse by keeping it firmly on the aids, reducing speed in the approach to the obstacles (especially uprights without a ground line) and going for a small, safe jump. You have to accept the fact that towards the end of the course the horse is not capable of jumping big and acrobatically any longer, and will have lost much of his ability to snatch up his forelegs quickly enough in emergencies.

Riders who have not yet competed in a tough three-day event may read this with some scepticism, but they must take heed if they do not want to meet their Waterloo one day in the last stretch of a long and demanding cross-country course.

CHAPTER 10 Staircases, Terraces, Walls, Ski Jumps, etc.

I have already dealt with the approach and jumping of parallels and uprights built on ascending or descending terrain, so let us now consider the technique of jumping up staircases, terraces, walls etc.

They must all be approached with a lot of impulsion, and because horses will slow down and engage their hind legs of their own accord when they see the obstruction, the rider does not have to check the speed; on the contrary, it may be advisable to increase it. The rider must then facilitate the powerful thrust of the hind legs and be quick to go forward with the horse.

Fit, fresh horses are capable of cantering without much difficulty up steep slopes where humans would have to crawl on hands and knees. Not realising this, well-meaning riders dismount at the foot of a stiff climb and this can, instead of encouraging the horse, make him apprehensive. Unless steady rain has made the ground bottomless, horses canter uphill with ease; they just need a confident rider and plenty of impulsion.

None of the terraces that I have encountered has been excessively difficult; some being bounces, others requiring one canter stride between the steps. If impulsion and take-off are accurate at the start, the rest of the obstacle is usually straightforward.

Refusals are most likely to occur when there is a small ditch at the base, but the problem the ditch presents is mostly imagined; the ditch is rarely more than 1 m wide, which means that the horse has to take off 1.5 m from the base of the bank. Nevertheless, riders can sometimes be so impressed by this small ditch that they will slow the speed and extinguish impulsion in the approach, with the end result that horse and rider come to a stop and are in danger of sliding into the ditch. Previous unhappy experiences play an important role. The horse may have been confronted with this sort of obstacle too early in his career, and,

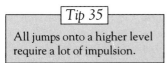

Tip 35

All jumps onto a higher level require a lot of impulsion.

having stopped a couple of times, been punished, thus establishing fear of the obstacle in his mind.

The only successful remedy is to practise frequently approaching these obstacles with full impulsion as if the ditch were not there. It is the rider who must train himself to ignore the ditch. Restoring a horse's confidence after a bad experience takes time and patience. The rider should ask less of him in training by jumping smaller obstacles of the same type, while maintaining impulsion – perhaps in the company of a lead horse. This applies of course to many other obstacles and situations. Confidence will grow with impulsion, and impulsion with confidence.

Jumping Down

I treat all downhill jumps and, above all, jumps into space, with considerable respect, but I have never had any difficulty jumping off banks. Horses always want to jump off them and at Kloppenheim, over the years, there have been surprisingly few refusals at the awe-inspiring ski jump. Even when a horse has

At the top of cliffs and ramps, the rider must press his fists into the horse's neck as if trying to push the horse downward.

refused once, it will never do so again. At Kloppenheim again, I have never had a refusal when the staircase had to be jumped from top to bottom. The all-important thing is to make perfectly clear to the horse the rider's intention to jump, neither too slowly nor too quickly. At Kloppenheim at the top of the ski jump the horse must be brought back to the walk before jumping into space but his desire to go forward must not be inhibited. The rider must remain seated and use his weight, hands and legs to encourage the horse to go forwards and down.

With young horses especially I have always found it helpful to press my fists down on their neck, as if trying to push the neck and the whole body downward. It is probably a purely psychological aid, but it has always worked.

The situation is entirely different when the horse has to jump into space over an obstacle placed at the edge of a bank. There are more refusals at this sort of obstacle than at any other. At a national championship, half the Hessian team was eliminated at an insignificant log pile at the edge of a small ramp. At a major international event at Achselschwang most of the refusals occurred where a tree trunk of modest dimension was placed on the edge of a small ramp.

The size of the obstacle cannot have been the cause of those refusals; I am convinced they were the fault of the riders themselves. It is the rider, not the horse, who knows the course. The rider must act promptly and determinedly to get the horse to jump confidently, even though the horse cannot see where he is going to land. The speed has to be checked to a walk and then the horse must be driven forward energetically with emphatic leg aids on a very firm contact with hands held rather high. In the last galloping strides, the horse must be held as if in a straitjacket. The rider must be mentally prepared for the leap into space. In a sense, the horse must feel pushed down into space by the rider's hands. The straitjacket effect is all important. The more the horse has been collected and the more determinedly he is urged forward, the less the chance of a refusal.

The difficulty of this sort of obstacle is obvious. The horse has to be emphatically slowed down, but then has to be just as emphatically driven forward with the brake on, so that he goes at the jump in short powerful canter bounds; this is not as easy as it sounds. If the obstacle is situated in the first part of the course,

---

Tip 36

Refusals are frequent at obstacles on a downhill slope because horses cannot see the ground on the far side. Riders must drive at them with determination keeping the horse positively on the bit.

When jumping over an obstacle into space, the horse must on approach, be collected to the point where it is like being in a straightjacket. The rider must collect the horse and drive him forward with impulsion, holding the hands high.

when the horse is still fresh and probably pulling hard, slowing him down and collecting him ('bending the bow') is not easy. Conversely, if the obstacle is at the end of the course, it may be difficult to maintain impulsion, to keep the horse sufficiently on the aids to obtain the short, bouncy canter strides required before the jump. Refusals are nearly always due to an imbalance between the horse's desire to go forwards and his submission to the aids. Frequently the rider will have failed to slow the speed in good time, and will then have to brake so hard that impulsion is completely destroyed. The very slightest hesitation on the part of horse and rider can guarantee a refusal.

We must distinguish between jumps into space situated on level terrain and those built on a descending slope. On level going it is much easier to check the speed; you can concentrate on the take-off and think of the landing afterwards. The horse's agility will usually ensure a safe landing, even if the approach was somewhat too speedy. It takes much more skilful riding to negotiate this type of obstacle when it is built on a downward incline. The tactics for a downward approach have been described before.

Drop Fences

Drop fences differ somewhat from the type of obstacles considered above; the drop is much bigger. They need special consideration because of the great likelihood of a fall if the rider makes a mistake. A typical example of a drop fence is the famous Becher's Brook in the Grand National at Aintree, where horses

Drop fences call for courage on the part of both horse and rider. The rider must resolutely impel the horse to jump forward and downward.

have to clear a massive hedge, on the far side of which there is a 3 m wide ditch and a further drop of 2 m. The reason why so many horses fall at this fence is that they jump too short and land on the edge of the ditch, so that they then have to gallop virtually uphill after landing. The falls do not occur at the precise moment of landing, but after the second or third stride when the horses have not been able to get up on their feet again.

The problem is the same at drop fences in eventing. The jump itself is usually not particularly difficult; it is the landing that is critical. So the rider should in this instance imitate the steeple-chase jockey and adopt the safety seat, that is the old English hunting style of seat in the saddle and body upright, or even leaning slightly backward. By thus unloading the forehand, the

At big drop fences, the old-English jumping, or safety, seat is preferable.

rider gives the horse the chance to get safely onto his feet after landing. The rider must also give the horse freedom to lengthen his neck and still maintain sufficient contact to enable the horse to use the reins as a balancing aid.

I have seen a horse stumble on landing at a moderate drop fence, turn a slow somersault and break its neck. The rider had maintained a forward seat, had not allowed the horse to extend his neck (hampered as he was in any case by a martingale) and had not offered him the balancing aid of a firm contact on a long rein. When to adopt the safety seat, and the degree to which the rider leans backward are matters that are frequently debated amongst event riders and there are some people who sneer at this old-fashioned way of riding. I shrug off the criticism; there are circumstances when this style is an advantage rather than a disadvantage. Remember safety first, especially at drop fences.

CHAPTER 11 Combinations

By far the greatest number of faults occur at combinations. They are the decisive stumbling blocks over cross-country as well as in showjumping; they really do sort out the wheat from the chaff. At the international three-day event at Achselschwang in 1986, 90 per cent of mishaps happened at one of the eight combinations. Almost half the number of competitors were eliminated, to my knowledge because of trouble at one of these combinations. But why do they cause so much trouble? Combinations demand fulfilment of two conditions:

1. The horse must have certain natural aptitudes and must be perfectly educated.
2. The rider must help the horse by organising the approach to the obstacle.

The Natural Aptitudes of the Horse

Temperament
It is at tricky combinations that a hot-headed horse spells disaster. There are always moments in every competition when the rider can give little, if any, assistance. In such situations, it is essential that the horse is on the aids, going in a relaxed rhythm and also clever at getting itself out of trouble. Combined obstacles are the end of the line for the puller and the impetuous jumper. The horse does, however, still have to be courageous and forward going. The hesitant horse that has to be driven every inch of the way is as much of a liability as the tearaway.

It is impulsion – sustained impulsion – that is essential to avert a stop in a combination.

Submission
Submission is mostly a matter of education, but it is closely linked with temperament. There are many horses that show submission in the dressage arena but cannot be controlled across

Having ridden a cautious approach to the first element, the rider must keep the horse firmly between his hands and legs, and ride strongly and directly to the next element.

country in the same way. However, there are many combinations that demand a high degree of submission, be they simple uprights that have to be met with absolute accuracy, V- and Z-shaped obstacles with angles that have to be jumped precisely, jumps into sunken roads that have to be approached slowly but require powerful forward drive on the way out, and, finally, combinations involving a 90 degree turn and therefore a very high degree of submission.

Combination fences in particular, therefore, require a naturally submissive temperament in the horse, a trait which is essential, not only across country, but also in the dressage arena. Without this submission the chances of success in eventing are remote.

Quick reactions
There are numerous combinations where a horse needs more than four legs. For example, at a bounce, the horse may hesitate and have to put in a short stride. It will need very quick reactions to find that extra leg that will avert a fall.

Much of this is due to education and training, but not everything. Big, powerful horses that tend to overjump are at a disadvantage. Conversely, thoroughbreds, that for centuries have been bred to jump 'flat', are more agile; like cats they are quick to bring a hind leg forward when they are in danger of losing their balance. An excellent example of this natural agility is Charisma, who, ridden by Mark Todd, came first in the 1984 Olympics.

Schooling Over Combinations

Nothing requires more perseverance and consistent schooling than the jumping of combinations.

Approach
As I see it, 99 per cent of the secret of faultless combination jumping lies in a good approach. I believe that nearly all refusals are due to insufficient impulsion in the approach to the first element of the combination.

The stars of our sport, like Horst Karsten, Virginia Leng or

Lucinda Green owe their success not so much to the natural quality of their horses, but to the rider's technique in the approach to the really difficult obstacles of a cross-country course.

We must not however confuse speed and impulsion. Jumps in and out of sunken roads, for example, call for a slow approach while maintaining impulsion in order to jump out of the road and clear the upright on the other side.

Rhythm

This brings us to the concept of rhythm. Only the rider knows what lies ahead. It is he who has to decide on the appropriate rhythm, and communicate clearly his decision to the horse. Most combinations are so designed that they have to be negotiated at a steady rhythm and speed. Successful jumping of the whole combination depends on correct jumping of the first element; if the first part is jumped properly, the rest will usually follow without trouble, and the rider can sit quietly without disturbing the horse.

However, at combinations built on an uphill slope, or with a wall or a ditch in the middle, impetus has to be developed after the first jump; but the latter must be approached with a lot of stored up impulsion, the rider driving energetically with seat and legs against a restraining hand.

On the other hand, it may be necessary to slow the speed inside a combination, for example, when a ditch is succeeded by an upright, or an oxer by a jump into water. This admittedly is much easier. Even an uneducated horse can be brought rapidly from a gallop to a walk or a halt; we need only watch a group of young horses at pasture, galloping towards a fence to see how quickly they can slam on the brakes to avoid running into it. But building up impulsion again once it is lost is very difficult. It is only possible if the horse is very well-educated, confident and forward going.

Confidence

I have said that it is essential to jump combinations frequently during training; this is in order to develop both the horse's trust in his rider, and the rider's trust in the horse. The obstacles must be constantly varied in their sequence, in distances between

Tip 38

The secret of successful negotiation of most combinations lies in the correct approach to, and jumping of, the first obstacle.

Tip 39

Too much impulsion at combinations is better than too little. It is easier to reduce impetus than to build up impulsion that has been lost.

jumps, and in dimensions and structure in relation to the contours of the ground. It is also important to include awkward distances provided the obstacles are low; they help to develop the agility of the horse and quick reactions in horse and rider. Bounces particularly need to be practised as often as possible but over obstacles of modest dimensions. They are the best way of developing mutual trust between the partners and of ensuring that, when confronted by more impressive obstacles of this type, the horse will tackle them confidently and surely. If you do not have wall combinations or coffins on your home ground, take the horse to some place where they are available for training. They are included in almost every horse trial above novice level.

The key to trouble-free jumping of combinations – apart from the right approach – is confidence instilled by years of experience. If a horse has been patiently trained to jump as many different types of combinations as possible without being over-faced and thus having imprinted on his mind the memory of frightening and painful experiences, he will tackle boldly difficult combinations in competition and will know how to get himself out of trouble in critical situations in which his rider cannot give further assistance. It is the jumping of combinations in competitive conditions that show whether, during training, we have given the horse the full opportunity to develop into a self-reliant partner.

Combinations are usually the determining factor on the cross-country course. These include jumps into water as well as walls, steps and sunken roads. All these jumps require careful inspection in order to assess the horse's likely reaction, and the correct action to be taken.

Tip 40

In the course of jump training, it is essential to ride as often as possible over as many different varieties of combination as possible.

Assistance by the rider

The greater the experience of the rider, the easier the task of the horse, but experience does not depend on the age of the rider or the number of events in which he has participated, it comes to the rider who:

- Carries in his mind a clear picture of the dimensions of a combination and its construction in relation to the terrain.
- Has carefully planned the approach to every combination and is capable of carrying his plan into action.

– Carefully observes as many other riders as possible at particularly difficult obstacles.

The Rider's Education

Since the jumping of combinations has such an influence on the cross-country results, here are some additional remarks and tips.

Success starts with training on home ground. Trotting over poles, trotting over poles with a cavalletti at the end, riding over a series of cavalletti, riding over cavalletti followed by one, two, three, four, five or six jumps, and varying the distances between the jumps: short bounces, long bounces, or related jumps with one or two strides of canter.

The rider must first teach himself to approach and ride through every combination at the same even rhythm and speed. Later he has to learn to build up or decrease speed between obstacles; this is much more difficult and at the beginning the obstacles must be kept simple and small but varied. These exercises must be repeated endlessly until they become second nature to horse and rider. In winter it is more convenient to carry out this very basic training in the riding school, but in the early days of spring the training must be continued and developed in open

These easily portable cavalletti can be built with three heights.

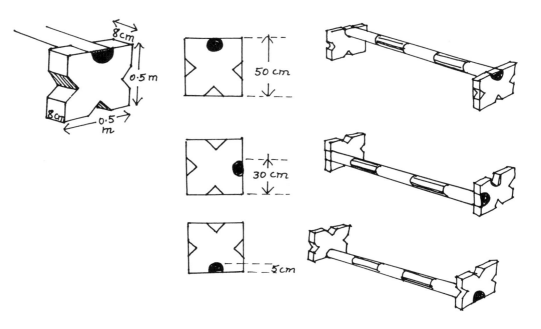

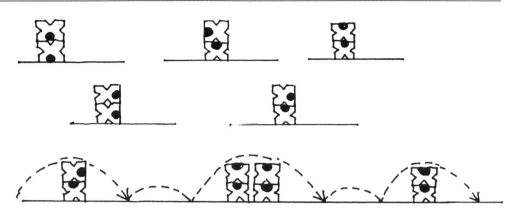

Cavalletti can be used to construct a large variety of combinations.

Tip 41

I make much use of cavalletti at home. They are so easily transportable that with very little labour you can constantly vary combinations and their degree of difficulty.

Tip 42

The event rider should train himself and gain experience by looking for, and taking advantage of, every opportunity to ride over the type of obstacles normally to be found on a cross-country course.

---

country. Every unevenness of ground, every contour difference of the land must be sought and used to practise upward and downward jumping. With the help of cavalletti and at the cost of very little labour it is possible to simulate jumps onto and off walls, a sheep pen, a jump over a road and combinations of V- and Z-shaped jumps.

I have used cavalletti for many years. They are built, to my own design, out of synthetic material for the poles and aluminium or plywood for the supports. They can be adjusted to heights of 10, 25 and 50 cm, and are so light that there is the added advantage that two can be carried at a time without difficulty. I know it is often said, and not without good reason, that event horses should be trained over obstacles as solid as possible; but for me the variety of obstacles to which I can introduce my horse with the help of cavalletti is a more important consideration.

As an active participant, I have not experienced another sport beside cross-country riding where it is more difficult to simulate at home the difficulties that have to be faced in competition. I must therefore improvise and create obstacles that are going to teach my horse to be agile, to react instinctively, to come back to hand, to extend, to motor on, to jump flat or to bascule, to jump at speed or from a standstill.

Since it is rarely possible to create a real cross-country course on home ground, you should, as often as possible, look for other places where more or less exact replicas of the real thing exist; showjumping courses and established cross-country courses. It is also important to ride as many other horses as possible.

I have been an event rider for ten years but, before that, I competed in showjumping for 20 years. Showjumping has taught me to judge distances, calculate take-off and determine speed, and that experience has been of enormous advantage in my new sport. I strongly advise other riders to take part in as many showjumping competitions as possible, with different horses, certainly at novice level, but even at medium level wherein the maximum permissible size of the obstacles is somewhat bigger than any to be met on a cross-country course. It is precisely for this reason that showjumping is such excellent preparation. The show-jumper who has regularly been faced with the big oxers and trebles that have to be jumped at medium level will not easily be overawed by the dimensions of those awaiting him on a cross-country course.

It is wonderful to have an equine champion that carries you bravely through thick and thin all the year round, but always riding the same trusted horse is an unprofitable exercise; eventually it leads to a dead end. When that horse has come to the end of his career will you ever be able to enjoy again the sweet taste of success? Horsemanship, that is the education and training of horses, is an art that can be acquired only by association with many different horses. A sufficient variety of conditions is equally necessary for the complete education of the event rider. If a rider has only the one good horse, the experience of riding in championships presents itself, at most, five or six times a year. I therefore strongly recommend that you should try to obtain as many outdoor rides on other horses as possible. Any opportunity to gain experience should be taken, be it in novice events or in the hunting field.

The essential thing, for rider and horse, however, is the opportunity to train over unfamiliar terrain and typical cross-country obstacles. If riders were allowed to use existing courses to train themselves and their horses, the quality of our sport would increase rapidly and the risk of falls and injuries would be greatly diminished.

There is one thing that I still do not understand. The cross-country phase usually takes place on a Saturday; the showjumping on a Sunday afternoon. Sunday morning would be a perfect time to take a young horse out on to the cross-country course and train over some of the best constructed obstacles. I am sure that

Tip 43

Get off home ground; go showjumping, ride different horses, and try to get permission to practise over unknown terrain and obstacles.

permission would nearly always be given if it were requested politely, but I have seen very few riders take advantage of this opportunity. How can we expect horses to go boldly at the type of obstacles they or their riders have never before been faced with? One reason why the British have dominated the sport for so many years is that they take their horses out of the riding school, go hunting, and can compete in numerous horse trials and point-to-points.

Elaborating on Jumping Combinations

I have already said that it is essential to plan one's course of action over every part of the course. This is particularly important in respect of combinations. The exact dimensions of the obstacles, the state of the ground on the take-off and landing sides, the contours of the ground, the foreseeable conditions of visibility, the position of the sun and the performance of other competitors; all these factors have to be carefully considered when formulating a strategy which has then to be committed to memory. With combinations, one must also take into account the ideal line to the next obstacle, possible obstruction by spectators and unpredictable circumstances.

Success or failure in the jumping of combinations depends a great deal on the planning of what the rider considers to be the ideal line for his horse and sticking to it. At Achselschwang in 1986 a very unfriendly looking birch oxer stood before the pond, and about a fourth of the field was eliminated there. I had decided on a rather circuitous approach which would bring me at a right angle to the oxer; the majority of riders had decided against this as being too time consuming, but I was proved right. Akki Bua jumped superbly over the oxer and then into the pond without any trouble.

I spent three days at Achselschwang pondering over the approach that would best suit Akki Bua. Time after time I measured the distance between the obstacle and strode back and forth over the line of approach. I measured the oxer carefully; at one place it was 1.2 m high and 1.6 m wide, at another it was only 1.05 m high and 1.4 m wide. The combination was at the end of the course. How tired would Akki be? It would be necessary to warn the horse of the approaching difficulty by slowing and collecting him; in doing so I would also give him a

A water combination at Achselschwang in 1986. A third of the competitors had refusals or were eliminated at this obstacle because they took the direct route (dotted line) and approached at too great a speed to negotiate the jump over the oxer (a) and then the steep jump (b) into the pond (c). The trouble free, though longer, route is indicated by the dashed line. The horse had first to be collected and then, while being kept positively on the aids, driven with renewed impulsion at the oxer.

moment to get his breath back. I talked to the horse to encourage him to slow down many strides in advance. We were both fully alert. We followed the planned route with absolute precision, and all went well, which goes to show that the right strategy for combination jumping cannot be learnt from books. There are too many factors to consider, many peculiarities that may apply only once, on a particular day, with a particular horse and in a particular situation. In addition, you have to foresee the presence of spectators; they always congregate at combinations, especially those involving a jump into water. They have not yet disturbed any of my horses, indeed a crowd of onlookers seems to stimulate Akki Bua to greater endeavour and make him more attentive. On the other hand there are many horses who shy at the sight of spectators and can easily be driven off course. It is therefore important for the rider to be extremely alert at those places and to ride determinedly with the most decisive aids.

There are always unpredictable circumstances and not every combination can be negotiated according to carefully laid plans. All I can say is that the rider must be aware that they exist, and be prepared to jump big or let the horse put in a short stride.

Combinations are a rich source of surprises, and you must be prepared for them; they demand special alertness and quick, instinctive reactions. I will illustrate this point with another example from Achselschwang, where a massive tree trunk lay at the edge of a deeply sunken road, out of which another log had to be jumped on the opposite bank. When walking the course I had not envisaged that this combination would be particularly

At this type of combination (Achselschwang 1986) drive, impulsion and rhythm must all be right.

difficult and my starting time did not allow me to observe how other competitors had coped. I could not know that those ahead of me had had a lot of trouble there, especially in jumping the second log. Quite unperturbed, we sailed over the first log and slid down the bank, when I suddenly heard the spectators shouting 'Go on!' so Akki and I drove on as if galvanised by an electrical prod with much greater urgency than we had intended; and thus we jumped over the second log easily.

CHAPTER 12 Water Combinations

Water combinations are the subject of intense discussion amongst competitors and the favourite gathering point for spectators because they are the most frequent cause of refusals and falls. The actual difficulty of jumping into water is often greatly exaggerated by talk before the event and by a certain sensationalism on the part of some spectators. This can result in negative riding which is almost bound to cause a mistake. By measuring the actual dimensions of a water jump with a yardstick, the rider will realise that it is not particularly high or wide. The only real or imaginary added difficulty is the water. Very patient training is necessary to accustom horses to step or jump into water. Touble-free jumping of water obstacles requires complete elimination of fear of water.

Accustoming Horses to Water

If you take up eventing, the one thing that has to be practised more than anything else is teaching young horses – and older ones also – to go through water. Bruce Davidson has said that if he has a horse that is frightened of water, he takes a book with him on a hack and makes his horse stand in water for hours. Horses instinctively distrust murky water of unfathomable depth; it could have hidden dangers. We have to persuade them that water is not dangerous, but that it is cooling and pleasant. They should learn that they can play in water, splash in it, wash out their mouths and even drink it. Horses must be taught to like, and to enjoy going into, water, so that, after frequent pleasant experiences of splashing about in it, they will jump into water fearlessly.

However, after the unpleasant experience of a fall into water the horse's confidence will have been shaken and the whole training process has then to be repeated as soon as possible. Even old, experienced horses should frequently be required to go through water and be reminded that it is not dangerous.

When horses are scared of water, you should, like Bruce Davidson, have a book to read while making them stand in the water for long periods of time.

To develop this essential fearlessness of water, I will, during training, repeatedly make a horse step in and out of it, and stand in it until he gets thoroughly bored. Horst Karsten says in his book that a young horse should first be ridden through water rather than be allowed to stand in it; this teaches him always to go forward. I, however, think that it all depends on the individual equine temperament, but, on the whole, feel that calmness and confidence are the most important things to develop, and letting a horse just stand in water helps to develop these. Of course with a young horse the bottom should be firm, the water relatively clear and no more then 20 cm deep. It is easier to persuade a horse to stand in still water but I have not experienced any great difficulty with running water. It seems that horses are less frightened of running water, which is usually clear, than of murky, stagnant pools.

The depth of the water is an important consideration and the more uniform the depth the better. Officially, a depth of more than 50 cm is not allowed but this rule is sometimes disregarded by the course builders. Horst Karsten would like to have this maximum permissible depth reduced to 30 cm and I think that he is right. After all a jump into water is intended only to prove a horse's total obedience to its rider; it should never be the cause of a fall.

It is probable that most falls in water are caused by a jump into an unsuspected hole in the bottom, the presence of which is only revealed when a number of horses in an event have fallen into the trap. This was the case at Fussgonheim and at the national championship at Luhmuhlen in 1985. Most of such totally unnecessary accidents would be prevented if a maximum depth of 30 cm were not exceeded. At Luhmuhlen I only avoided a soaking because I had seen a rider falling in the water and I was able to choose a different place from which to jump into it.

Development of Agility

Development of the horse's confidence is the first aim in training the horse to jump into water. The second aim is the development of its agility. The horse has to learn to overcome the strong braking effect of the water. As always, training has to be progressive, and the demands at the beginning must be minimal; going through shallow water first at the walk, then at the trot, and finally at a collected canter. I never canter on carelessly in water but always discipline myself and train my horse to concentrate and pick up his feet. The horse must be on the aids, as if doing the passage, and never be allowed to go through water on a loose rein. To this end, I will eventually drive him through various depths up to 80 cm or 1 m. Every horse must at some time have learnt to move through such depths and the rider made to feel the powerful braking effect. Water can suddenly check speed and distance with the force of a blow. The deeper the water, the more cautiously and slowly you must jump into it and ride through it.

Tip 44
Always reduce speed significantly before jumping into water; when trotting or cantering through water, the rider has to concentrate and must keep the horse collected.

Gymnastic Jumping

To accustom the horse to changes of speed and jumping into water, we must make him do gymnastic jumping: in the approach to water, into water, out of water and finally over an obstacle after water, as he will frequently have to do in competition. In preparation for major national or international events, we must improvise and practise all sorts of water combinations. At Luhmuhlen, Badminton and at the World Championships at Gawler in 1986, for example, none of the jumps into or out of water were very big but they all demanded a high degree of obedience, rhythm and powerful impulsion.

Jumping Into Water

The most difficult part of a water combination is the jump into the water and you should simulate at home as many different types of water obstacles as possible. Start by jumping over a cavalletti into shallow water from the trot. You could of course build a bigger jump of say a maximum height of 1.2 m and a breadth of about 1 m, but the most important thing in jumping water is building up the horse's confidence and when it comes to training him to jump this type of obstacle, demands should always be considerably reduced. In my experience, a small bounce jump into and out of water over cavalletti is much more useful for developing rhythm and confidence than a jump directly into water. Jumping out is a more simple affair because of the horse's and rider's natural desire to get out of water as quickly as possible. Loss of impulsion and concentration with the horse coming off the aids will result in difficulties. It is, therefore, advisable to build a small obstacle at the edge of the water on the far side, this can later be developed into a bounce or a simple combination.

Approaching water at speed and jumping big into it is a mistake; a rather cautious approach with the horse under control is advisable.

Cavalletti can be used to build all sorts of jumps into water, in the water and out of water.

Finally the horse will have to be trained to jump over small obstacles situated *in* the water. On the whole, riders seem to exaggerate this difficulty. A horse's instinct is to get out of water as quickly as possible and to do so he will usually jump obstacles that are in the way. This natural drive also helps in the case of a bounce from water into water. The risk then is of the horse jumping at too great a speed into the second part of the obstacle. Always remember to consider the strong braking effect of water on speed and length of stride. You should, therefore, never aim at jumping big into water; the smallest jump possible is preferable. The same applies to cantering in water where it is much more difficult for the horse to lift up his forehand than on firm ground. Speed must be reduced as much as possible to allow the horse to make short, bouncy strides. In many cases it is even advisable to jump in and out of water from a concentrated trot.

Tip 45
Never jump big into water; come at a concentrated trot or a short, bouncy canter.

Correct Riding at Water Jumps

Although most falls at water jumps are caused by a hole in the ground below the water, a good number are due to incorrect approach. All jumps into water necessitate a slowing of the pace, sufficient collection, rhythm and positive rein contact.

I do not know of a water jump that requires an increase of

When cantering in water, never canter across it in long, flat strides (above), keep the horse as collected and calm as possible (below).

speed in the approach. On the contrary in 99 cases out of 100, speed must be considerably reduced, this makes the horse more attentive, gives him a breather, allows the rider to put him back on his hocks, and softens the impact with the water. Feeling more secure in this abnormal element, the horse is more likely to remain calm and not fumble. Almost all jumps into water can be taken from the trot but there is then a risk of refusal. On the whole it is better to approach at a collected canter.

If the horse is suitably collected about 20 to 30m before the edge of the water, a refusal is unlikely. Water combinations usually come at the end of a fairly long stretch of fast galloping, when horse and rider are running out of steam. These jumps have to be ridden with as much concentration and renewed impulsion as other combinations and, consequently, this waning

Obstacles built in water rarely cause any trouble if the horse is collected and working with impulsion. The impulsion is helped by the horse's natural desire to get out of water as quickly as possible.

The horse's natural desire to go forward also facilitates jumping out of water. He must remain collected, however, and not be allowed to get 'strung out' while in the water. The rider should aim for as small a jump as possible out of the water.

energy may cause many refusals at water. Water jumps are critical obstacles; they make great demands on horse and rider and can only be negotiated if the horse is properly collected and they are never taken at speed.

Germany is undoubtedly the homeland of dressage and dressage training. Riders are taught to sit up and keep their hands low. Who dares to tell them that when riding across country they may have to hold their hands high at certain obstacles? Yet this practice is essential to jumping into water; about 20 to 30 m before the obstacles, the rider must sit up and establish a firm rein tension with hands held rather high and well apart. The upright seat naturally necessitates a somewhat long length of

rein, but the horse must be collected and driven strongly up to the bit with the rider's seat and legs. It is only by holding the hands rather high that the rider can ensure a precise liaison with the horse's mouth and control each canter stride. The wide distance between the hands has a stabilising effect on the horse; it allows the rider to sit deeply and to incline his body either backward or forward as the situation demands. It is also very advisable to make a single or double bridge with the reins.

Supporting the horse with bridged reins is something that has to be practised frequently on home ground and it is just as well to do so under the eye of an experienced horseman. The rider must not lose his feel; on the one hand he has to be capable of

A big jump into water can easily result in a fall.

collecting the horse firmly, and, on the other hand, he must maintain impulsion and go with the horse over the jump. It is an art perfectly exemplified by the top American show-jumpers and by Nelson Pessoa who are justly admired as much for their stylishness as their success. Photographs and films show clearly that their ability to ride with such fluency and precision over a course of formidable obstacles is due to a large extent to riding on a long rein with hands held rather high.

Sitting Out the Landing

The matter of rein length brings us finally to the subject of the landing in water; the critical moment of the jump. Many falls in

When jumping water combinations, the rider must sit upright with the hands held high and wide apart which helps stabilise the horse. The horse must be collected and driven forwards strongly with the seat and legs.

water are caused by bad riding. It is not usually at the moment of hitting the water that the horse falls, but in the next one or two canter strides. This is because, as when jumping down from a height, the horse has not been able to regain his balance after landing. Here also, the old English style of jumping, which unloads the forehand, should be adopted. The firm rein contact enables the horse to use his neck as a balancing aid and enables the rider to help lift the horse's head quickly after the initial impact with the water. Short reins and the forward, weight-relieving seat, make this assistance impossible; the rider is much too busy struggling to maintain his seat.

Falls in water are never due to too slow an approach, but to too fast an approach, neither are falls due to a rider leaning backwards excessively, but to an insufficient backward inclination. At water the motto must be: safety first!

CHAPTER 13

The Sunken Road and the Coffin

The sunken road and the coffin are obstacles usually made more difficult by being immediately preceded and followed by another relatively high obstacle. The greater the difference in height and depth between the obstacles forming the combination, the more difficult it is. An additional problem is that many horses experience a moment of fright as they jump over the first obstacle and suddenly catch sight of the deep ditch or coffin over which they next have to jump.

As with all combinations, you have to consider the most time-saving way of jumping sunken roads and coffins, and, most

Akki Bua and the author jumping in to a combination in a flat, economical style of jumping.

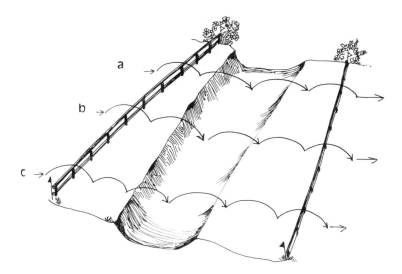

A typical sunken road: (a) is the quickest but riskiest route using four canter strides, and (c) is the slowest and safest route using six canter strides.

importantly, the maintenance of impulsion both in the approach to the first part of the combination and between the obstacles.

The Sunken Road

There is a large variety of combinations of this type – comprising a void between two more or less higher obstacles – the whole combination having to be negotiated either as bounce jumps or with, at most, one intervening canter stride between the jumps. This distance problem is compounded by the already mentioned 'moment of fright'; the slightest flinching by the horse on take-off can result in quite a predicament for the rider.

The Coffin

In German, the coffin is called Pulvermann's Grave. It is an obstacle that was conceived for the first time in the Hamburg Jumping Derby after the First World War by the enthusiastic course designer and hunting rider Eduard Pulvermann. The Hamburg Jumping Derby has lost none of its prestige and is still considered to be one of the most formidable showjumping courses in the world. Pulvermann liked to include in his courses the sort of obstacle that would be encountered in the hunting field, for example, there was one where you had to jump a fence out of a paddock, then, after one stride of canter, jump a ditch, and finally, after another canter stride, jump a fence into a paddock situated higher up. It is recorded that at its first experience of this obstacle. Pulvermann's horse stumbled and threw his rider into the ditch. Hence the name Pulvermann's Grave. This story is a good example of what I have called the 'fright factor'; the horse sees the ditch just before jumping, or even while jumping, the first obstacle which can cause him to stumble.

In the Hamburg Derby, Pulvermann's Grave is made even more difficult as the ditch is filled with water; the sudden sight of this causes many a startled horse to knock down a pole. It is a combination that requires great control in the approach and a high, well arched jump. Of course, the cross-country rider does not have to worry about knocking down poles, but his horse startled by the sight of the ditch may shy violently and suffer, at least, a severe loss of impulsion, if not a fall.

| Tip 47 |

Be prepared for the 'moment of fright' that causes the horse to flinch when it first notices the coffin.

Inspecting Sunken Roads and Coffins

The 'moment of fright'. Just before taking off the horse may see something unexpected and frightening. The rider must be prepared for this and drive the horse on energetically as soon as he feels him falter.

When walking the course, the rider must inspect a sunken road or coffin most carefully in every aspect. Should the obstacle be approached directly, exactly in the middle, or to the right or left, or would an approach at an angle gain more space? In my own experience it is better to slow down some distance before the obstacle, to give yourself more room for collecting the horse, and then to drive forward energetically. Slowing down and 'fiddling' at the last moment gives the horse even more time to stare and waver. If the first obstacle is negotiated without loss of impulsion, the rest is usually an uncomplicated matter. It often pays to decide on an indirect, more time-consuming approach, a short jump and an extra canter stride. Almost all horses, especially if they have no previous knowledge of a course, will instinctively shorten the stride when jumping downhill over a ditch. They

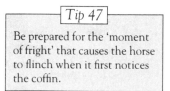

Jumping off a wall with the horse perfectly on the aids.

will also tend to get well under the obstacle on the way up and out of the combination because they cannot see clearly the ground on the other side. There are few cases when taking the shortest way, jumping long and flat, and negotiating the whole combination in as small a number of strides as possible has proved to be good policy. I have seen more than one well-known and successful partnership coming to a stop or a fall at this sort of obstacle because the rider had apparently not given it sufficiently serious attention when inspecting the course.

It is particularly important to consider the differences in height of the combination parts. Is the landing going to be on a slope or on level ground? Will increased impulsion have to be produced to negotiate the ditch or the sunken road or would the impulsion previously acquired be sufficient to carry you through?

For the sake of safety, I prefer to have the horse collected on approach with a lot of stored impulsion which can be released explosively at the right moment, but it is sometimes necessary to approach at speed. If you are not certain of being able to build up, contain to the last moment, and then release a large quantity of impulsion which will carry you safely through the whole combination; it is better to choose the shorter, speedier route and rely on speed in the approach.

Observing Other Competitors

It can be much more instructive to see how other competitors cope with the sunken road or the coffin than to pace the distances repeatedly and work out a theory. Horses see things through horses' eyes and have the instincts of horses. My reckoning that a distance of 4 m between the ditch and the end obstacle can be negotiated in one bounce by my horse may have to be revised after watching how other horses manage to put in an extra short stride. It may be because of the condition of the ground on that particular day, the situation of the combination in the middle or towards the end of the course, the contour of the terrain or some peculiarity of the obstacle. I know that my horse could jump it as an in-and-out but I have been warned. It is, unfortunately, rarely possible to be able to observe personally how other competitors manage at difficult obstacles, but information can be obtained from other observers and the groom can often feed this back to the rider before the start. It can also be useful to find out how the combination was jumped in previous events. You may choose to ignore the advice or example of others, but they interest me and there is always something to learn.

The Approach

Quite some way from the obstacle I bring the horse back to hand which gives him time to assess the situation and gives me time to develop the canter rhythm I have planned for jumping the first part of the combination. I may have to talk loudly to the horse to get his attention and encourage him to slow down. I shorten the canter strides, sit firmly, and close my hands on the reins, holding them rather high and well separated, to collect the horse as much as possible between hands and legs before the jump. I

Jumping the coffin combination demands a concentrated, determined approach, maintaining sufficient impulsion to negotiate all three obstacles.

Training

aim for as modest a jump as possible and avoid inclining my upper body forward too much or lightening my seat because I must always be ready to sit down and drive on again in order to maintain impulsion. The rider must already be looking at the last obstacle and concentrating his thoughts on it as he is going over the first. 'At all combinations, one must ride for the last obstacle'; wise advice because impulsion has to be maintained until the last obstacle of the combination has been negotiated. However, in the case of the sunken road or the coffin the manner of jumping the first obstacle requires great attention; remember that you have to bear in mind the 'fright factor' and be ready to urge the horse on energetically the moment one feels him faltering. As I have already said, if all goes right at the first obstacle and impulsion is maintained, the rest is relatively easy.

Sunken roads and coffins demand a considerable measure of agility on the part of the rider. Within the space of a tenth of a second he has to change from a forward, accompanying seat, to a deep, driving one, thereby staying as close to the saddle as possible. A deep seat helps to preserve the balance of horse and rider, gives the horse confidence and therefore helps to maintain impulsion. Moreover in critical situations – as when a horse stumbles or unexpectedly puts in a short stride – only a deep seat enables the rider to help the horse to keep or recover his balance by unloading his shoulders. A rider who hangs onto his horse's neck for support cannot help the horse.

It is absolutely necessary to train the horse at home to jump combinations like the sunken road or the coffin. A very small ditch will do, and with the use of cavalletti you can vary extensively the height of the obstacles and the distances between them. For the coffin, a simple piece of tarpaulin can be used to make the ditch look deeper and more daunting; cheap plastic sheeting at the bottom can give the appearance of water. It is rather more difficult to simulate convincingly a sunken road. However most riding schools will have a 'billiard table' or a bank, and, again, with the addition of cavalletti it is possible to reproduce to some extent the sort of combination likely to be found on a cross-country course. The important thing is to develop fluency and a steady rhythm. The 'fright factor' cannot, of course, be simulated in these exercises as easily as the obstacle, but as trust develops between rider and horse, so should the horse's self-assurance, and the first time he has to jump over a proper coffin in strange surroundings, he will do so just as fluently as during practice despite the probable intrusion of the 'fright factor'.

CHAPTER 14 Steps and Banks

I like steps and banks more than all other obstacles; they always seem to belong to their surroundings, even when they have been built purposely just for one particular event. They should be tackled boldly, at the regular, rhythmical, energetic canter characteristic of the experienced, confident hunter used to going over uneven terrain. In fact it is here that our sport comes closest to its hunting origin. These sort of obstacles are, moreover, a singular aptitude test for horse and rider. The rider has to ride at and over them energetically, purposefully and fearlessly, and to be able to give his horse all the assistance he needs when jumping up or down. The rider must also be extremely agile.

Good rhythm and impulsion are required to jump up steps, and both horse and rider need to be extremely agile.

Tip 50

The jumping of ascending
steps requires enough
impulsion to last to the top.

When working the horse at home it is essential to give him a
lot of practice at canter at and over obstacles of this type until he
jumps without pause or hesitation. They are seldom tests of
exceptional courage but they do require a high degree of nimble-
ness and almost cat-like suppleness. The ability to maintain, and
even increase, impulsion over the series of steps and to put in an
additional stride if necessary is very important. Many bank combinations and ascending steps demand increased impulsion after
the first step. However with the help of cavalletti and a modestly
sized bank it is quite possible to give the horse the necessary
experience on home ground.

Steps

Ascending steps
Springing up a series of steps demands principally impulsion,

like all jumping of combinations, but there are two peculiarities about this kind of obstacle. Firstly, I must store up enough impulsion on the approach to be able to reach the last platform without exerting myself unduly. I must also be in a position to obtain renewed impulsion at the foot of the last step when the initial impulsion will almost certainly be waning. Many steps have to be taken in a series of bounces which makes it difficult for the horse to regain impulsion between each step. Secondly, the same fright reaction as that induced by the sight of the coffin combination can be expected, sometimes because a small ditch may have been dug at the foot of the staircase, or simply because of the daunting appearance of an ascending succession of walls. Unless a ditch has been built at the foot of the first wall, it is better to plan a close take-off and a short jump; this makes for a better arching of the jump onto the next step. Moreover it gives

Bold, powerful, rhythmical jumping up steps.

the horse a better chance of landing well forward on the first platform which makes jumping onto the following levels easier. It is very important to measure the jumps carefully when walking the course. If a bounce on level ground is measured at 3 m, then to negotiate easily a series of jumps onto a higher level, you must work to a measurement of 2.5 m for each individual jump. All steps with platforms of 3 m or more require serious consideration. Should they be taken as bounce jumps, or would it be better to reckon on a small intervening stride? When coming to a decision, you must take into account the state of the ground, the height of the steps and also the location of the obstacle, i.e. whether it is at the beginning or the end of the course. At the beginning of the course, the horse is still full of zest and should be able to ascend the steps in a series of bounce jumps; at the end of the course, much of this zest and power will have been considerably dissipated and one may have to choose to put in a small intermediate stride between each leap.

Descending steps

When jumping down steps you can happily canter at a normal speed provided that the various levels are of the same size and that you do not have to jump over a tree trunk or a pile of logs at the top of the descent. In this latter case, the greatest caution should be exercised. Many horses will stop unexpectedly because they cannot see the landing spot.

Some steps are natural features of the ground with or without the adjunction of specially built obstacles. At the Pheasantry at Wiesbaden, for example, you have to jump over a series of tree trunks placed on a fairly steep slope and, after the last one, with just one intervening canter stride, over a sizeable parallel. The difficulty is compounded by the fact that the distances between obstacles are not constant. Here total collection and concentration are called for and the ideal line has to be carefully considered when walking the course. On steep slopes, as with all obstacles, my motto is always 'safety first'. I never let the horse 'roll down' and thus come off the aids. To avoid this risk I am not too proud to choose the longer way.

To negotiate obstacles erected on a descent, you must approach slowly, at a collected canter, or even at a trot, but without losing impulsion. The parallel at the bottom of the

Jumping down steps: the rider demonstrating to perfection the highly advisable 'safety' seat.

Pheasantry at Wiesbaden is particularly instructive because it can only be cleared if impulsion and collection are maintained from the top to the bottom of the slope. There is a similar sort of obstacle in the Hamburg Jumping Derby, although it is much more difficult. It is the famous white plank, 1.6 m high, which has to be jumped 8 m after the end of the descent of the steep Derby wall.

Banks and Walls

Banks and walls come in an even greater variety of forms than steps, but the one thing that they have in common is the

Good embankment jumping. A relatively short jump, the rider going with the horse and keeping it well between hands and legs. A lengthening of the rein helps the horse to find its balance as it jumps down.

necessity for impulsion. Small earth banks and walls may sometimes be jumped with the forward seat but I always prefer to sit down for a short while; it makes me feel safer and it is then easier for me to recover control of the horse after jumping off the bank. A loss of impulsion is usually the failing of young, inexperienced horses or riders who are lacking in confidence and boldness. This is why it is so necessary to practise jumping small banks from every possible direction as often as possible at home. One should bear in mind that jumping off banks into space does severely jolt the horse's forelegs. Ideally the practice bank should be higher on the approach side than on the jumping-off side, thus demanding good impulsion for the jump up, and allowing sufficient slowing down before the smaller jump down. With young horses

especially I jump a lot of small banks from the trot; gymnastically it is excellent work and important for the development of strength of the hindquarters. These sensible exercises also develop the horse's boldness and from a bold horse I can obtain impulsion – and preserve the impulsion obtained – without unduly exerting myself.

The big Reitdamm (embankment) at Achselschwang clearly demonstrates the importance of this gymnastic work at home. It is situated in a dimly lit wood and so looms before you quite suddenly. At the foot of the embankment there is a very narrow ditch. You have to jump a height of 1.2 m to get onto the top, then about 3.5 m further on you jump over a 1 m high log pile into space to land on a counterslope at a much lower level. Many riders were eliminated there in 1986 for refusals either at the foot of the bank or at the log pile. This obstacle needs to be approached boldly, with a lot of impulsion but without allowing the horse to extend himself too much; the rider must aim at a short but powerful jump onto the top of the bank and one stride of canter before jumping the log pile. You would have to be riding an extremely bold and powerful horse to dare to treat this combination as a bounce.

I mention this particular obstacle because it is a good example of two basic difficulties associated with banks. One is that the horse, on catching sight of the soaring wall, will slow down of his own accord; the rider must urge him on, not only to prevent a refusal, but just as importantly to 'bend the bow' without, however, slowing the horse down. He must use seat, legs and hands to make the canter more bouncy, more powerful. Holding the hands rather high (as I have already explained) ensures a positive contact with the horse's mouth, better determination of the stride length and, therefore, of the take-off point. The second difficulty is that on the top of the embankment the horse must be able to put in a short stride promptly before jumping over the rick into space. He will be able to do this only if, at that moment, the rider sits deep, and bundles up tightly the horse's power before releasing it for the jump over the rick and into space. I use the expressions 'bending the bow' and 'bundling up the horse's power' to stress that situations such as this call for extremely positive riding. The horse must trust and obey the rider implicitly; only the rider has advanced knowledge of the magnitude or difficulty of the obstacle, but the rider must help the horse, and to do this he must truly 'work' with his body and mind. It is my impression that at the Reitdamn at Achsels-chwang, most of the refusals could be attributed to the riders. Furthermore I believe that about half the number of refusals in horse trials, from novice to intermediate, are also the fault of the riders. It is in the hope of being able to help to reduce this proportion of refusals that I have compiled this collection of tips.

At Kloppenheim there is a little bank on top of a hill that used to be an uncomplicated and enjoyable obstacle that you could take easily in your stride, until someone thought of making it much more difficult by building a small rick on the bank. To enable a horse, which usually would be fairly extended, to bas-

| Tip 52 |
Ride at a collected canter into a bank as if it were a true parallel; work energetically with the legs and seat and hold the hands rather high.

cule neatly over this rick, he had to be collected after he had jumped onto the bank. At Luhmuhlen, the combination consisted of first a 0.6m high wall, followed by another wall with a ditch in front of it, then by a hedge and ditch, then a third wall and finally a second hedge, and a big jump into space at the end. This particular combination is a good example of the necessity of deciding in advance on the ideal personal line. With a very forward-going horse you can approach at the right side which gives one canter stride between obstacles. If the horse is shorter striding, you should come from the left side which allows for two canter strides between them. At Luhmuhlen, in contrast with Achselschwang and Kloppenheim, it is important not to lose momentum. The combination is less difficult and the whole can be negotiated in a series of smooth, rhythmical hops.

Training

I have come full circle back to the beginning of my thoughts about banks and steps in general. Basically they are the easiest of the various forms of combinations and in any case the most enjoyable ones to ride. However it is absolutely necessary to have, at home or elsewhere, the right training facilities and to practise frequently. The demands on the horse should be modest at the beginning: the smaller the better. You can approach from the trot or the canter, but, in both cases, with the proper amount of impulsion. Confidence grows out of impulsion, and confidence fosters the maintenance of impulsion.

CHAPTER 15 Ditches

Thinking back on all the different kinds of obstacles and all the cross-country courses over which I have ridden, I have realised that the one imperative which applies as much to the jumping of ditches as to the jumping of all other sorts of obstacles is impulsion. When jumping ditches, impulsion means an increase in the basic rate of the canter, i.e. more kilometres per hour. In showjumping the rider starts to accelerate three or five canter strides before the water jump, but, leaving it so late in cross-country would require a sudden expenditure of energy which would disturb the rhythm and, most importantly, could well extend the horse too much and disunite his canter. The cross-country rider must demand an almost imperceptible, gradual increase of speed over a distance of 30 to 50 m before the obstacle, and attain optimum speed several strides before take-off. The rider can then sit and drive with legs and seat, while maintaining rein contact with hands closed, but well apart, and held rather high. This is not to slow the horse down, but to get him to engage his hind legs even better, in order to develop more powerful strides prior to take-off while maintaining the speed acquired.

This is the way to ride at ditches which are always long jumps, but sometimes, like Trakehners, they combine length and height. Many horses experience a moment of fright and will hesitate before jumping over a ditch. It is to avoid this risk that it is essential to develop momentum over a sufficient distance and to have the horse well on the aids in the last strides.

> ### Tip 53
> Horses normally hesitate before jumping ditches. To avoid this, speed must be built up over a good distance, and in the last strides before take-off the rider must sit and hold the horse strongly between the legs.

Dry Ditches

Dry ditches on the whole are pretty straightforward affairs. Remember that the length of an average canter stride is 3.5 m, but at a strong cross-country pace it can be more than 4 m. In major showjumping competitions, the water jump is usually 5 m wide and the riders use a very limited number of strides to build up sufficient speed for the long jump. In open country, ditches are seldom wider than 4m and so, in size, they are not formidable obstacles. However, their difficulty can be enhanced by certain peculiarities which have to be studied carefully when the rider walks the course.

Is the take-off point distinctly indicated?

If the take-off point is clearly indicated, it is much easier for the horse to notice the ditch and to estimate its size. Frequently, however, there is no such indication and it is the rider who has to make the best arrangements he can to help the horse clear the ditch. He will have examined the ditch carefully when walking the course and will have decided whether it can be more or less hopped over or whether it is a really long jump. He will then have to relay this to the horse as effectively as possible.

What is the state of the ground on the far side?

I once had a fall at a ditch because my horse could not cope with the difficulties posed by the steeply sloping terrain and tree roots on the landing side, followed by a bend in the course. This proves how carefully you must examine every obstacle. On that occasion, in view of the trickiness of the ground on the far side of the ditch, it would have been better to approach at a slightly slower speed.

The situation of the ditch

The most difficult ditches, whether they be dry or filled with water, are those situated on a slope, in a depression in the ground, or between high banks.

A famous example was the notorious 'fascines and moat' at the Berlin Olympic Three-Day Event of 1936. The jump was over a broad water-filled moat dug deep between two sloping banks. It was not possible to jump over the ditch from the top edge of the bank; the only possible way to clear it was to put in a very short canter stride on the side of the bank and then to take off boldly from the edge of the water and leap powerfully onto the opposite bank. This meant that the pace had to be distinctly slowed down, and the horse sufficiently collected to enable it to make a long, high jump. There are a number of similar ditches that are part of a combination requiring that powerful long, high leap.

Tip 54

Some ditches are situated after a turn or on a bend, it is, therefore, important to be able to obtain increased impulsion on bends as well as on the straight.

The angle of approach

There are many cases of ditches that are not situated at the end of a long straight run, but shortly after a turn or on a bend. It is therefore very important for the rider to develop the ability to obtain increased impulsion on bends as well as on the straight. This amounts to lengthening the trot or the canter on a circle. Why then do so many riders struggle so hard to slow down their horse on the bends only to have to drive on frantically in the last few metres before the obstacle? As I have said before, the right way to ride a bend is the way of the skilful motorist who brakes before the bend and accelerates into it.

Water-filled Ditches

Wonderful impulsion and extension.

All that I have said about dry ditches – regarding the presence or absence of a distinct take-off line, the ground conditions on the landing side, their situation in relation to the contour of the ground, or the angle of approach – applies to water-filled ditches.

The author's mother, the first woman to take part in horse trials, at the Munich event in 1931, using considerable impulsion to negotiate the cross-country course.

However, water shines, reflects light and ripples and the fright factor has again to be contended with when jumping water-filled ditches. You must therefore ride at them with even greater determination and impulsion.

Ideally the horse ought to be able to see the water from a distance and thus be prepared for the jump, but when the ditch is at the bottom of a depression in the ground or on a bend, the horse will see it only at the last moment. It is then up to the rider to prepare the horse and to forestall hesitation.

The rider can get the horse's attention with his voice or with a slap on the neck, but he must sit up and urge the horse on in good time with energetic aids.

Fortunately there is not the worry, as there is in showjumping, of incurring a fault because a hind foot touches the tape at the edge of the water jump; all that matters is that the horse does jump and that our safeguard against a refusal is, once again, impulsion.

Sunken Ditches

A ditch situated at a lower level than the surrounding one, a Trakehner for example, is rarely a particularly difficult obstacle. The difficulty for horse and rider is really an optical illusion. If the rider allows himself to be overawed by the superstructure – perhaps an oxer – he may slow down too much and induce a refusal as the horse suddenly notices the ditch, or the horse may get caught on the oxer. Horses will always stop at water if they are held back, yet neither should it be approached at excessive speed because this will encourage the horse to elongate himself too much. It would be too difficult to keep him on the aids and get him to tuck his hind legs under him for a well arched jump over the fence. All sunken ditches must be approached with great impulsion but the horse must be strongly compressed between legs and hands by energetic riding.

This sort of combination is particularly difficult to negotiate when it happens towards the end of the course, when the horse is tiring and getting longer and longer. I therefore plan to give him a recovery pause, and for about 10 seconds, over a distance of approximately 100 m, I let the reins get longer and stop driving. The canter strides become slower and quieter, but at least 100 m before the critical moment, I must take the horse in hand again and ride energetically to restore impulsion.

> ## Tip 55
>
> Sunken ditches are not particularly tricky obstacles. The difficulty for horse and rider is mostly an optical illusion. You must ride at them boldly with increased impulsion.

Training for Ditch Jumping

The more patiently and progressively you train a horse to jump ditches, whether dry or full of water, the quicker the horse's confidence grows. The moments of fear at the first sight of water will become shorter and shorter.

When training a young or inexperienced horse over water, I always use an experienced lead horse. Initially, I follow the lead horse, then we ride and jump abreast, and finally the lead horse follows me. There is nothing better than a good lead horse to build up the confidence of a young, inexperienced horse, and to help him lose his instinctive fear of ditches and water. Quite often, when following the lead horse, the young horse may become impatient and start pulling and running at the ditch. This does not worry me unduly. The horse is learning that all ditches have to be approached boldly in a forward-going manner and with great impulsion.

CHAPTER 16 Alternative Routes

Obstacles with alternative routes have considerable spectator appeal, which is a good thing for the sport. Designing them imaginatively and intelligently is a challenge for the course builder but they are just as much food for thought for the rider. The two factors that have to be pondered over are risk and time.

The Risk Factor

It is when first walking the course that the rider must carefully study the different ways of jumping an obstacle with more than one route. For example an oxer may be difficult for the horse, but still easier than a bounce of uprights. There are four things that have to be considered:

1. The size of the fences and the distance between them.
2. The capability of the horse.
3. The state of the going.
4. The location of the obstacle; at the beginning, in the middle or at the end of the course.

Measuring size and distance
It is not always worth considering an alternative route. The difficulties of each obstacle can be so different that all riders choose to go the same way. At Luhmuhlen in 1983, after the birch fence, the riders were presented with a choice between the direct route over a difficult bounce or the longer, circuitous one over several uprights. All riders without exception chose the longer way. One should therefore give serious thought to an alternative route only if it has serious advantages that outweigh a little loss of time.

The capability of the horse
The capability of the horse must then be taken into account, which is more difficult than taking the measurements of the obstacles and the distances between them with a tape measure.

Tip 56

The younger or more impetuous the horse, the more cautious should be the choice of approach to the combination. The most important thing is to maintain rhythm and impulsion.

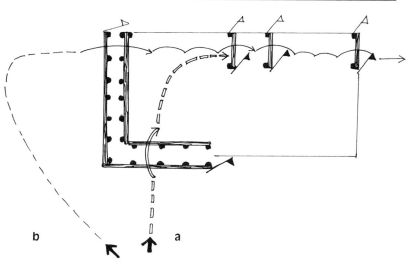

When there is an alternative route over a combination, before deciding on the shorter way, you must evaluate the risk carefully. Can you trust the horse sufficiently to be able to choose the shorter but more difficult route (a) or play for safety and decide on the easier one (b)?

With a young horse or an impetuous one, it is wiser for example to take the longer way ending over an oxer than the shorter way involving a zig-zag and a bounce. With a seasoned, sober horse one can unhesitatingly approach at an angle and predict that it will easily cope with a succession of bounces.

The state of the going

It is of the utmost importance to foresee a possible alteration of the going. For example, what may have appeared to be firm going at the time of inspecting the course may have been transformed into a morass, through which one will have to wallow, after a downpour of rain or when thirty or more preceding horses have poached the ground badly. A straightforward bounce of 4 m can then be transformed into a very tricky one. In such conditions, the essential impulsion needed to tackle a big oxer will suddenly fail you and even if it entails a substantial loss of time you must go for the easier of the options.

The location of the obstacle; at the beginning, in the middle or at the end of the course

I have mentioned this factor in several chapters. It is one of the most important ones that the rider has to consider when he plans his overall strategy. Whenever a series of obstacles – combined obstacles, walls, alternative routes – has to be jumped, you have to predict the condition of the horse at that stage. Will the horse still be too keen, too impetuous, too excited, or, on the other hand, will it have become spooky, hesitant, tired, strung out, out of breath, or clumsy? With Akki Bua, when approaching the middle of a course, were there an alternative, I would confidently take the shorter route over a sizeable oxer, but towards the end of a course I would decide to go the longer way, over a series of uprights, giving the tired horse the opportunity to put in a short stride between obstacles. Of course the right way could be the complete opposite with a different horse. There are horses that become longer and longer without losing their jumping power and, with them, towards the end of the course I would find it easier to go the short route over the parallel. There is only one rule – and like all rules it has its exceptions – which is: it is only after they have jumped a few obstacles that horses loosen up and get into their stride. As regards alternatives, one should wait patiently for this moment before choosing to go for the option that demands the most impulsion and stretch. This is usually towards the middle of the course by which time the horse will have unwound and be at the top of his form. Towards the end of the course, however, you must always decide on the safest alternative; at this point the principal aim should be to get home in one piece.

> **Tip 57**
>
> When deciding on which option to choose when there is an alternative route over an obstacle, it is important to predict the condition of the horse at that moment. Will he still be too tense, will he have got into his stride, or will he be tiring?

The Time Factor

We can now consider the time factor, that is, how much time can be gained by going for the shorter though more hazardous route. Simple calculations will prove that the risk factor should always be foremost in your mind when deciding on an option. By choosing the shortest way, I may gain perhaps 10m, perhaps 30m. At a speed of 500m per minute this amounts to 1 or 3.5 seconds. I could easily gain this amount either by slowing down later in the approach to some obstacles or by pushing on hard after a jump. However, as I have already said, the alternative route is sometimes as difficult as the direct one, and when this is the case the important consideration is maintaining rhythm. Every deviation from the straight line costs time and effort: the horse must first be collected and then urged on again. A large number of alternatives are either a straight line over a series of obstacles – sometimes a series of bounces – or a slight detour leading over only two oxers. With an experienced horse, I would always go for the more direct way. I know that many of my fellow competitors would decide on the longer way with the fewer obstacles, reasoning that it is the jumping that takes it out of the horse. I cannot agree. I believe that even if it entails jumping a series of obstacles in quick succession, sticking to the straight line is much less tiring for the horse than a change of direction, after which it has to exert itself to regain speed.

The Approach to Alternatives

Another factor to take into consideration when making a choice between two options, is the ease of approach. As I have stated about combinations, if the approach is right, the first obstacle in a combination will most probably be negotiated correctly, and the major difficulty will have been overcome. Thus if I have to choose between two equally difficult courses, I will be influenced by the ease of approach to the obstacles on the way. For example, even if the obstacles were slightly bigger or slightly more difficult, I would go for the way that offered the easiest, safest approach, that is the one requiring the least alteration of direction and speed (rhythm).

Particular Alternatives

Parallel or upright?
Once again it depends on the horse and on the location of the combination (at the beginning, in the middle or at the end of the course). I must say that I do not like big true parallels and given the choice I would rather go for the upright or the succession of uprights, although a parallel at the exit of a combination is not so difficult if the previous obstacles have been easily negotiated. Rider and horse can more easily get one another out of trouble at uprights if things go slightly wrong.

Corners
Whether to go for the middle of the uprights or for the corner will depend mostly on which option offers the most direct route. Of course the horse must have been properly trained at home to jump over corners; if he has, the jumping of corners in competition is often easier than it might seem at first. However, one should never venture to jump over a corner if the horse shows

123

Tip 58

The saving in time when there is an alternative route can be a secondary consideration. Risk is the more important thing to bear in mind.

the slightest tendency to run out. He must first learn to go perfectly straight at all obstacles.

Water

Quite frequently, one of the options is to go through water. Now it takes double the time to canter through water than on solid ground. This certainly does not mean that one must invariably decide on the other option. Again it is the risk factor that must decide the issue. Safety first. In the end it is better to lose some time than to run the risk of being eliminated.

A jump out of water onto an islet or platform over an obstacle and back into water involves such an expenditure of energy and so great a disturbance of rhythm that you should contemplate it only if your horse is extremely experienced. In any case all alternatives involving water need to be pondered over seriously. Time permitting, watch how other competitors cope, it will help you come to a decision. If a particular alternative has been jumped before, listen to the experiences of others, they too can help you make up your mind.

Alternative ways of jumping a swing bridge. The first rider has chosen to jump from the unfinished bridge and the second rider has decided to go through the water.

CHAPTER 17 The Showjumping Phase

Tip 59

The standard of showjumping in major horse trials is bound to be set higher in the future. It is therefore essential to train your horse just as carefully for this phase of the competition as for the others.

Although the showjumping obstacles do not make bigger demands on horse and rider than the cross-country ones, this phase must not be treated light-heartedly. A knock down which could have been avoided by greater concentration is infuriating if it costs you relegation to a lower placing or perhaps a win. But it is my impression that bigger or more intricate courses are, very probably, going to be built in the future for national or international championships. The days are long gone when the showjumping phase was merely a test of the horse's fitness at the end of the competition. Like the dressage test the showjumping is going to have an increasingly decisive influence on results. There are two good reasons why this should be so. First, out of consideration for our partner, the horse, you cannot go on devising ever bigger, more demanding cross-country courses. Well-publicised fatalities in the last few years are spoiling the image of horse trials. Therefore the only way to increase the difficulty of the competition is to set higher standards for the dressage and the showjumping. I remember that in the 1986 World Championship at Gawler none of the first eight competitors incurred any penalties in the steeplechase and the cross-country; the issue was determined by the score in the dressage and the showjumping. For example, the young British rider Anne-Marie Taylor riding Justyn Time with three faults in the showjumping slid down from third place to fifth. Consequently the showjumping phase will have to be considered much more seriously in the future.

The second reason is that the participants in the sport, both equine and human, are becoming increasingly proficient. Many eventing horses nowadays are such good jumpers that they would not be outclassed in a showjumping competition at medium level.

And so, to retain the lead in a tight competition in a three-day event, a clear round in the showjumping is essential. The things to be considered are:

1. The actual difficulty of the course.
2. The condition of the horse the day after the cross-country.
3. The nervous stress on the rider.

The Actual Difficulty of the Course

In novice horse trials, the obstacles in the showjumping will measure 1.1 m to 1.2 m. To accustom the horse to jump obstacles of this height, one should regularly take part in beginners' show-jumping competitions (Newcomers) or even at Foxhunter level. The important thing is that the horse should have been confronted with true parallels before having to face them in the showjumping phase of a horse trial. The latter ought always to be easier than those in showjumping competitions which have been entered to give the horse experience. However showjumping courses at Grade B and C level are pretty formidable nowadays and I can see little point in training the event horse up to such a standard.

Akki Bua and the author at Achselschwang in 1986. Despite a careful approach, the horse hit the front pole of this oxer lightly with a foreleg and dislodged the pole. This mistake caused their relegation from fifth to seventh place.

Tip 60

The inexperienced eventing horse should be taken to as many different showjumping venues as possible; he must be trained to jump over coloured obstacles at a collected canter and must be given regular jumping practice in beginners' classes.

How often one goes showjumping must depend on the experience of the horse. An inexperienced horse should be trained to jump coloured obstacles and be taken to as many different showjumping venues as possible to get him used to the atmosphere, the crowds, the sounds, the colours of the obstacles, and to all those things that in the showjumping arena are so different from those of cross-country. However, with an experienced eventer that no longer gets flustered in a showjumping arena, it is not advisable to subject him to the extra strain, because every competition, every obstacle jumped, whether over a cross-country or a showjumping course, shortens the life of the horse's limbs.

If the horse regularly baulks at a particular type of obstacle, at a water jump surmounted by coloured poles for example, I would on the whole prefer to take him to some private training establishment and train him there in peace and quiet. Eventually it is important to enter into some competitions in which the particular type of obstacle has to be jumped in more difficult conditions than those found at the training establishment.

We must never overlook the fact that designers of the showjumping course in horse trials will usually try (in Germany) to introduce one or more 'natural obstacles' such as a water-filled ditch, a Trakehner, or a coffin, to which the horse must be accustomed during training. The penalty for a refusal is too high; it means losing all hope of finishing close to the top.

The Condition of the Horse

The final phase of a three-day event takes place the day after the horse has endured two stretches of roads and tracks, a steeplechase and tough cross-country course.

Your course of action on the day will depend on the condition of the horse. Some horses will still be tired and stiff, they may need a long, gentle warming up period. I favour gymnastic jumping over quite small obstacles, from the trot or from a relaxed canter. It may be necessary, finally, to ride once over a higher obstacle and let the horse knock down a pole just to remind him to be careful. In the meantime you can also give him a short, sharp canter to wake him up. Considering the time prescribed of 400 m per minute (it is 350 m per minute in a novice class in showjumping) the number of horses that incur time faults is surprising.

Tip 61

Even if my horse appears to have recovered completely from the exertions of the previous day, I must prepare him for the final phase of the event with great patience and consideration, allowing him plenty of time to warm up.

Even if the horse appears to have recovered completely from the exertions of the previous day and does not appear particularly stiff or tired, you must still allow for a long and careful warming up period. First a long period of walking, then some trotting alternating with walking, and finally some gymnastic jumping from the trot. It is my experience that older horses especially, however tired they may feel on the day, rise to the occasion splendidly when they hear the bell, proving once again that horses cannot be treated as mere instruments of sport. It is truly this final phase of the event that best demonstrates the quality of the relationship established between horse and rider. In the preparation and carrying out of this phase, the rider for his part, must listen to his partner, have sympathy for him and treat him with all the consideration that he deserves.

Nervous Stress

Finally we have to consider the nervous stress. It is made worse by the fact that the start is in reverse order of placing. Those at the bottom are the first to go. I always study the course most carefully, going over it several times. In my showjumping days I rode over more formidable courses, nevertheless, I measure the distances in my own strides with great care, and not only those between related obstacles. I study angles of approach, the position of the sun, the conditions of the ground, and especially the last obstacles. Even in ordinary showjumping, they are the critical ones, but on the last day of a three-day event I must foresee a possible loss of impulsion and zest due to fatigue or soreness of limbs following the stresses of the previous day. This intensive study of the course, as well as the long period of warming up helps to soothe the nerves. I watch the performances of the competitors who precede me, but avoid talking to anybody and letting anybody worry me. Nobody can help me now. As on the first and the second day, at this decisive moment I am alone with my horse. A condition of a successful round is total concentration of the mind on the state of the horse, and on the course and its possible stumbling blocks. My nerves are then not given any time to play up.

> **Tip 62**
>
> Study the course as seriously as if it were a Grand Prix. Careful preparation and total concentration of the mind on the task are the best possible assurances of cool nerves and a successful round.